GW00367650

THE MITCHELL BEAZLEY

POCKET GUIDE TO

DOGS

THE MITCHELL BEAZLEY

POCKET GUIDE TO
DOGS

SUSAN EGERTON-JONES

MITCHELL BEAZLEY

This book is dedicated to my mother and to my aunt, the late Daphne Jack, to whom I owe my love of animals.

Edited and designed by
Mitchell Beazley Publishers Limited
14-15 Manette Street, London W1V 5LB

Art Editor: Christopher Howson
Illustrators: Graham Austin, David Holmes, Susan Robertson, Pip Shuckbrugh, David Ashby Richard Lewington, Josephine Martin and George Thompson
Editor: Alison Franks
Typesetting: Kerri Hinchon
Production: Ted Timberlake
Executive Art Editor: Nigel O'Gorman
Executive Editor: Robin Rees

ISBN 0 85533 863 6

The publishers have made every effort to ensure that all instructions given in this book are accurate and safe, but they cannot accept liability for any injury, damage or loss to either person or property whether direct or consequential and howsoever arising. The author and publishers will be grateful for any information that will assist them in keeping future editions up to date.

The author and publishers would like to thank Bill Edmunds and Teresa Slowick of the Kennel Club of Great Britain, W.J. Jordan, M.V.Sc., M.R.C.V.S., M.I. Biol. of Care for the Wild, Judith E. Douglas, B.V.Sc, (Hons) Syd., M.R.C.V.S., and Betty Powell for their invaluable advice and assistance in the preparation of this book.

Text film by Mitchell Beazley in 8/9 point Garamond Book, and 7/8 point Garamond Italic
Origination by Mandarin Offset, Hong Kong
Produced by Mandarin Offset
Printed in Hong Kong

CONTENTS

Introduction 6

Introduction

This book can help you choose a dog, but cannot tell yo
which one you should have. That depends on you
whether you live in the country or in the city, how mu
time you can spend exercising your dog, how much yo
can afford to spend on food, and a thousand other facto
that limit individual choice. What we have tried to do he
is present the facts in an easily accessible form, that a
particularly relevant to selecting a particular breed or typ
sex, and age of dog, and then to consider in some det
what the dog requires from you, its owner.

You may already be attracted to one particular breed
dog or to certain types of dogs, but it is all important at th
stage to be totally honest with yourself about how mu
time you have available to look after it, the amount of spa
in your home, and your level of tolerance and patience
discipline and train it to be a happy, sociable member
your own immediate family and of society. The failure ra
in dog ownership is tragically high, usually because the p
has not fitted in with its owner's lifestyle, or with the famil
or perhaps with other pets. So never purchase a puppy c
impulse; think carefully, weigh up all the pros and cons a
bear in mind that you are taking on a full-time responsibil
for 10 to 15 years or longer.

If, however, you are prepared to feed your dog proper
train it patiently in the early days, take it for exercise in a
weathers every day of the year, correct or encourage
when it has deserved it, nurse it when it is sick, the
whatever sort of dog you choose, you will have
wonderful companion, and your dog will have that ra
breed – a good owner.

History

Wolves of varying types and
sizes were distributed over a
much wider range of the
earth's surface than they are
today, and although debate
continues on exactly how
the domesticated dog
evolved, there is no doubt
that the wolf was its
ancestor. Remains of dogs in
North America, India, Asia, **The Wolf**
and Europe have been found dating back to around 9,00
years ago. These would have evolved from the wolve
indigenous in those regions and, once the association wit
early man was established, selective breeding for preferre
qualities would have begun the process of producin
recognizably different types.

The likely pattern of development is that the Nort
American wolf gave rise to the Eskimo dog, the Chines

Chinese Temple Dog

wolves to the Chow and Pekingese types, the Indian wolves to the Dingo, Pariah, and the Greyhound and other sighthounds, and the European wolves to the Spitzes, Sheepdogs, Mastiffs, Terriers and Maltese. Trade, wars, invasions, and the nomadic movement of people over thousands of years inevitably led to further crossbreeding so that today it is impossible to trace the true ancestry of any of our recognized breeds.

Dogs are natural scavengers, and it is easy to surmise that their ancestors found the scraps thrown out around the settlements of early man very attractive. They would have accompanied their human providers on hunting expeditions when their skills in tracking, scenting, killing and guarding would have been highly valued, and from that point it was but a short step to harnessing those talents and identifying individual dogs most amenable to training.

The dog-human relationship is unique. The instinctive canine pack behaviour and organizational patterns of obedience, loyalty and adaptability respond well to human dominance. Humans, in turn, have used their dogs as companions and as workers in a wide range of roles: herders, hunters, guards, carriers, hauliers, guides. . . the list is endless and sometimes not very edifying. Dogs have also been bred for their meat, their coats, to fight as a sport and to be used in scientific research and experiments. The extraordinary variety in the appearance of dogs today reflects their long association with the whims and needs of man. Size, coat, physical attributes and temperament have been bred in and bred out; mutations such as dwarfism and taillessness have been promoted; and distinct types, breeding true, have emerged. It is only since the middle of the 19th century when the first dog shows attracted great crowds, that many of these types began to be classified into pedigree breeds with rigorously applied rules on physical conformity.

Dogs that have been bred for centuries solely as companions and pets may be more demanding, others bred specifically for certain types of work such as hunting may be more independent, but the description as "man's best friend" has been well earned by these animals that have shared and played a significant part in our history. There are more non-pedigree than purebred dogs in the world, and the evolution of dogs continues alongside that of man. We will continue to include them as much-loved members of our families, we will continue to use them to work for us, and I fear that some of us will continue to abuse them.

Which Dog?

THE PEDIGREE BREED GROUPS

Hounds

These breeds go back a very long way in history to the tim
when man first discovered that dogs could assist in th
chase. Hound breeds have evolved in almost every corne
of the world. They all have an inbred ability to track prey
some by scent and some by sight. Most have a high turn o
speed and considerable endurance. Their hunting instinc
can prove a distinct disadvantage to the pet owner, as onc
on the scent, or with their prey in sight, they can ignore a
commands to return to heel. But some breeds have now
become very popular pets because of their strikin
appearance, and generally sociable and characterful natures

The sighthounds, also called gazehounds, include th
Greyhound, the Saluki, the Afghan, the Irish Wolfhound, th
Borzoi and the
Whippet. All these
breeds are charac-
terized by a long,
slender   build
which equips them
well for hunting
fast prey. The
Whippet, which
has been called
"the poor man's
racehorse", was
developed in the
north of England
to course and race
by those who had
neither the space
nor the money, to

*The long, athletic lines of the Saluki or
Gazelle Hound are typical of the ancient
Middle Eastern hunting dogs.*

maintain a bigger sighthound. Small sighthounds like th
Whippet and the tiny Italian Greyhound have sweet nature
and make good pets.

The scenthounds were mainly bred as packhounds, an
few are suitable as pets except for the experienced owner
However, a few breeds have become very popular, notabl
the Basset Hound, the Beagle, and the Dachshund. Thei
obstinacy when on the scent can be controlled by using th
leash. However, they do tend to be rather vocal.

Gundogs

The dogs in this group were trained not to catch and kil
prey, but rather to assist with hunting – flushing out game
retrieving game and marking game. The breeding of these
dogs, and their continued popularity, was stimulated by the
invention of the gun. In the British Isles and in Nort
America particular types of dog were developed for a singl

8

purpose, while in other countries all-purpose breeds were more popular. The setters, pointers, retrievers, spaniels, Weimeraners, and Viszlas all fit into this group and all the breeds have proved very successful pets. Even the recently developed Kooiker dog of Holland is fast gaining popularity. None are suitable for city life except the small varieties, because of their need for a considerable amount of exercise. However, their easy temperament, their obedience, and their qualities with children have made virtually all the members of this group popular pets. They do need to be well trained from the start as many of them are large, heavy and exuberant.

It is a sad fact that their very popularity has ensured that they can suffer from hereditary problems caused by injudicious breeding. Hip dysplasia is one of the most common and most distressing. If you are buying any of these dogs, whether puppy or adult, make sure it is given a thorough check by a reputable veterinarian.

Working Dogs

This group covers a very wide variety of dogs that have been bred primarily to herd – sheep, cattle, pigs and goats – in countries all over the world. Differing terrains, climates and physical demands have given us the Old English Sheepdog as well as the Corgi and much in between. The main characteristics all share are hardiness, adaptability, acute eyesight and hearing and a quick intelligence. Often used to guard herds as well, the typical herder is large and powerful.

The natural intelligence of even the largest of the sheepdogs makes them easy to train. However, they do require very responsible ownership and are not necessarily the ideal pet. Their natural herding instinct – a joy to watch in working trials – can be easily mis-

The dense, long coat of the Old English Sheepdog covers a strong, working dog.

interpreted applied to a group of children and quite frightening. Also, they can become overpossessive of their owner if they are not taught to be sociable with both people and other animals at a very early age. The coats on some of these dogs can be quite a daunting prospect too! Hip dysplasia can be an inherited problem with the German Shepherd dog, so make sure your puppy is well checked.

Other Working and Utility Dogs

This is a very diverse group of breeds, also called non-herding dogs, rather dominated by the Mastiff types bred for

Mastiff

battle and guarding, but also including the Dalmatian, the Poodle, the increasingly popular Tibetan breeds and the Schnauzers. The Mastiff types all have the typical large square head, square muzzle, heavy weight and strong build, and some – the Rottweiler is just one example – have shown clearly in recent years that dogs bred for specific purposes can make very troublesome and sometimes dangerous pets. These dogs demand professional handling, and when they get it can make rewarding companions.

Probably the most popular pet breed in this group is the Poodle which comes in three sizes. Originally, the Standard Poodle was bred as a retriever, often for wildfowling, and it does love water. It is a large dog, light on its feet and, like its diminutive versions, the Miniature and the Toy, is full of character and intelligence. It has a dense coat that should be clipped, though without going to show extremes.

The Tibetan breeds that in recent years have gained so substantially in popularity as pets – the Shih Tzu, Lhasa Apso, Terrier and Spaniel – were developed as pets, guards or to assist in worship.

Terriers

This group is generally the most recently developed. As the Latin source of their name (*terra* – earth) implies, their purpose was to tackle and put up underground quarry. Medium to small in size, strong and square in stature and normally with a tough weatherproof coat, they are quick, active, independent, noisy and attractive little characters. They make excellent housedogs, but should always be kept under control with children even when they are used to them as they have such quick reactions. The Bedlington is the most unusual looking in this group and, indeed, owes its shape to the Whippet. But its character is all terrier. The Bull Terrier and the Staffordshire Bull Terrier were both bred to fight, and the Staffordshire used to be kept in the coal mines to keep down the rats. They owe their continuing popularity today to their devotion to their human families, children and grown-ups alike. They do, however, need firm, early training and socialization with other dogs as they are

Cairn Terrier

rong and have powerful jaws. The American Staffordshire
not as generally popular as its British cousin. A larger,
ore aggressive dog, it demands control at all times. The
ven bigger Pit Bull was bred as a fighting machine and is
otally unsuitable as a family pet.

he Spitz or Nordic Dogs

his group is easily defined by its appearance. The rather
road forehead offsets a sharp, pointed muzzle, and they
ave sharp pointed ears on a head that is alert and erect.
he dogs' coats are generally of medium length with stand-
f hair frequently forming a ruff around the neck, and the
ils are curled over the back. Mainly of medium to large
ze, they are quite heavy and very sturdy, and even the
iniature Spitz types are remarkably hardy.

Most of these dogs come from the regions around the
rctic, and include the European Spitzes and some
iniature varieties. They
ere, and many still are,
sed for sledge hauling, as
urriers, and for herding and
unting. The Siberian Husky
a typical example of a
orking Spitz, and the
amoyed is a good example
f a Spitz dog that is now
r more popular as a pet

Siberian Husky

an a worker. Friendly, active and intelligent, some of
ese dogs do make good pets and housedogs, and are
etter at coping with city life than most other large dogs.

oy Dogs

some countries this group of dogs is known as Small
ompanion Dogs, and in many ways this is a better
escription than Toy with its connotations of innate
laythings. Many of these dogs are miniatures of larger
reeds and it is an oddity of pedigree breed classification
orldwide that some appear in the groups of their larger
rethren, while others appear here. Miniature dogs bred
mply to be pets have a long history, and their survival as
e most popular range of pet dogs reflects their
telligence, high spirits and happy temperaments.
veryone will have their own favourites among the breeds
this group and they are well suited to a life in the city,
ough when you see a Pekingese hurtling around with an
ish Wolfhound in the wide open spaces of the
ountryside, it is a salutary reminder that these little
reatures are just as much dogs as their larger cousins. It is
orthwhile to check out the background of a pedigree Toy
uppy very carefully for strains that have been overbred.
n example of this is the Pekingese where some lines have
een developed with over-protuberant eyes which can be
asily dislocated.

CROSSBREEDS AND MONGRELS

The difference between a crossbreed and a mongrel is easy to define. A crossbreed is from known pedigree stock but of different breeds. In a mongrel at least one of the parents is of unknown stock. It is worth remembering that all the ancestors of today's registered pedigree dogs evolved through either accidental or purposeful crossbreeding to combine wanted characteristics and temperament. It can be fun to have a dog bred from parents of different breeds to see how its appearance and behaviour reflect those of its parents. You cannot know exactly what such a puppy will grow into, but you can make educated guesses based on your knowledge of the two breeds. Good breeders of crossbred litters will aim to provide in their puppies the best qualities of the parent dogs. It doesn't always work out, but the results are always interesting. Guide dogs for the blind are often bred by crossing a Labrador and Golden Retriever for instance, and another popular cross is the Lurcher which derives traditionally from crossing a Collie and a Greyhound to produce a fast, strong, coursing dog that will also respond quickly to command. (A cross between two or more sighthounds and maybe something else is known as a Long-dog.) When buying a crossbred puppy you should check out its parentage and its breeders as carefully as you would a pedigree.

Mongrels are popular pets.

Mongrels are often just as successful as pets are purebred dogs, and there is no shortage of them. If you acquire your puppy from the owner of the bitch, you will certainly be able to check out the character and physical appearance of the mother up to a point, but the father could be of any shape and temperament. It is just as important, though, to consider the conditions in which the puppies are being raised, and the health of the bitch. If these are satisfactory, the puppies have a good chance of being satisfactory too. But it is unwise to buy a puppy from a pet shop or a puppy dealer however appealing the pups, for there is no sure way you can properly check these animals or the conditions under which they have been brought up.

Many prospective dog owners are primarily interested in giving an unwanted dog or puppy a good home. Animal rescue centres have a wide choice of dogs, and good centres give the animals careful health checks, and quite often will insist on neutering them as well. These dogs may come from caring homes, but many have had bad experiences in their formative weeks, and these

sychological wounds can take a great deal of patience and
olerance to heal.

BITCH OR DOG?

ou should carefully consider the sex of dog you want. As
general rule there is little difference in character between
ne sexes in the smaller dogs, though the male can
ometimes be a little over-sexed. In bigger dogs both sexes
an experience cyclical mood changes, and the male can be
nore aggressive. Usually, an unspayed bitch comes on heat
wice a year – though some breeds such as the Basenji only
nce – and during the bleeding phase has to be confined,
which can be a bit unsettling for a pet as it seems like a
unishment. Hormone tablets or injections are available
om veterinarians to take a bitch off season, but anti-scent
blets are of doubtful use. Bitches can be quite disobedient
t these times and local dogs troublesome. The best way to
olve the problem may be to have the bitch spayed – unless
ou want her to have puppies. Male dogs can also be
resome to control if there is a bitch on heat in the
eighbourhood, and they can be inclined to wander. An
ver-aggressive or wandering male is often more
ontrollable if castrated. Neutering a pet, whether pedigree
r mongrel, while it is still young is becoming much more
ommon amongst owners who don't wish to show, breed
r be landed with unwanted litters. The operations are
raightforward and the outlay in money and in a little extra
oving care is generally well spent.

If you do want to keep your dog or bitch entire, then
onsider what the predominent sexes are of the dogs who
equently visit you or that live in the neighbourhood. Two
rritorial males, even if one is only visiting, can easily get
to a tiresome argument. If you are surrounded by
eighbours with entire bitches and decide to have a dog,
ou could find you had a pet that was less interested in you
an the attractions nearby.

PUPPY OR ADULT?

he advantages of having a puppy are that you can enjoy
l its stages of growing up, select the puppy you want,
sure that it is well looked after, and discipline it from an
arly age. (At 10 to 12 weeks a puppy is at the important
age when its responses to human control and relationships
e imprinted for the rest of its life.) The disadvantages are
at you must be prepared to spend a good deal of time
ith it, housetrain it and be very patient as it moves
rough the sometimes destructive stages of growing up.

The advantages of taking on a grown dog are that it is
sually housetrained, and, perhaps the main one, that you
e providing a home for an animal that for good or bad
as been rejected by a previous owner. The disadvantages
e that you are taking on an unknown quantity in terms of
arly nutrition, bad habits, training and discipline. Retraining

The decision whether to adopt a grown dog or a puppy should not be taken without considering carefully the advantages and disadvantages.

a grown dog demands very considerable patience and firmness and often, if it has been previously mistreated, a lot of understanding. And if the dog is large you will need to have some physical strength to keep it under control. Sometimes fear and bad habits persist through no fault of the new owner. Often, however, a grown dog makes a wonderful companion and family dog.

SIZE AND WEIGHT
When deciding what sort of dog you would like to own, two of the most important factors to consider along with looks, character and so on are its adult size and weight. A surprising number of people do not feel that a dog is a dog unless it is at least the size of a Labrador. What's conveniently forgotten is that a large dog not only demands quite a bit of space in the home, a good sized and secure garden or yard, and most of the back seat in the car, but also needs miles of exercise every day in every sort of weather, has an appetite to fit its bulk and is strong. Most of the large breeds have been bred for hard work – hunting, herding, hauling, and retrieving – and their physical and psychological fitness is dependent on their owners providing substitute "work" for them to do and the essential victuals for them to do it. This costs time and money – do you have both?

Training a large dog demands a fair amount of physical stamina as well as continued patience and tolerance – even taking a dog to training classes means giving up an afternoon or evening for several weeks. A well-trained dog should not pull on the leash, but even the best-mannered can become exuberant and if you don't have the strength to get it back under control, what then? Disillusionment, recrimination, legal actions, and possibly worse, risk to other people. So, it's important to work out what your weight/strength limit is. Try lifting the equivalent weight of the adult dog in a sack of potatoes, and you will then have a rough idea of what you can manage. Remember that your dog may occasionally need bathing – could you get it in and out of the tub?

The height of a dog is not necessarily a good guide to its weight. Compare the elegant Saluki with the sturdy Bull Terrier – there is very little between them in weight and a marked difference in size. Even some of the small dogs such as the Pekingese and the Dandie Dinmont Terrier are heavier and stronger than they look.

Dogs can be damaged if they are picked up incorrectly, and certainly children should be discouraged from picking up puppies unless the child is sitting on the floor and the puppy put into the lap. All too easily muscles can be strained and young bones dislocated.

Dog owners must be able to control their dogs in and out of the home, and a well behaved dog whatever its size is a delight to watch. All dogs love to be greeted and to greet their families even after short absences; but if elderly relatives are knocked off their feet as the two friendly paws of your Irish Setter land on their shoulders this is not the dog's fault, but yours, because you have not properly taught it how to behave.

Honesty with yourself is essential if you and your dog are to live healthily and companionably together. Following fashion or giving in to preconception can prove an unhappy experience – fair neither to yourself or your dog.

APPEARANCE

Your own personal taste in a dog's appearance – whether as an adorable puppy, or as an adult – is one of the key factors in your final decision on what dog you buy. In fact it is never a good idea to buy a puppy because of its appeal unless you are fully aware of what it will grow into, but you should take into consideration the amount of time you will have to spend on maintaining your dog's good looks. Both the quality and quantity of dogs' coats vary widely, and in the pedigree breeds this is easy to see. At one end of the scale you have the Chinese Crested Dog with little more than a tuft of hair on its head and tail; at the other the Komondor that is virtually hidden under the long, shaggy strands of its very thick coat. In between you have the smooth coat of the Weimeraner, the rough, coarse coat of the Cairn Terrier, the double, weatherproof coat of the Labrador, the long silky coat of the Spaniels, the curly, non-shedding (generally non-allergenic) coat of the Poodles,

The amount of time it takes to maintain a dog's coat depends on its length and texture as well as environmental factors.

15

the long, fine coat of the Yorkshire Terrier, and the wi
rough coat of the Irish Wolfhound.

Dogs with smooth coats need the least attention, thou
they should be brushed or rubbed down with a cham
leather every day. All the others need more attention: tho
with long hair such as the Old English Sheepdog or t
Silky Terrier have to be brushed and combed daily if th
are to be kept clean and their skin is to stay healthy, a
this can take a long time. Poodles are certainly happie
their coats are kept clipped back to a manageable length
though you don't have to go to the extremes seen at d
shows. Rough-coated terriers are more content if har
stripped or trimmed during the hot summer months. All t
care means a commitment from you of time and mon
and at least reasonably easy access to a dog parlour.

Remember, too, that longhaired dogs can be pretty sme
when they get wet and their coats can take quite a time
dry. In winter months, if there is snow and ice about the
dogs that have long hair between their pads can suffer fr
hard little balls of ice forming on their hairs which c
become quite painful unless speedily dealt with.

Apart from the Poodles, all dogs to a greater or les
extent shed their hair and will moult toward the end
winter. This factor is really the only one to bear in mi
when you are deciding on the colour you prefer. The pa
the hair, the more it will show up on clothes, on furnitu
on carpets, and in the car, and it doesn't make all that mu
difference if you have a smooth-coated dog or a longhair
one except in the quantity of hair shed.

Anyone buying a pedigree dog is well advised to che
thoroughly the breed "standard" beforehand. This will
guarantee exactly what your dog will look like, but v
provide a detailed summary of what to expect.

CHARACTER

All the pedigree breeds we know are descended from
wolf – and share many wolf characteristics. The reason
the large variety of breeds is that humans have selectiv
bred dogs to develop certain character traits and physi
points. A good dog of its breed, therefore, should repres
in its behaviour, looks and performance the dominant ge
that have been so carefully bred in to it.

In choosing a breed, it is important to assess what sort
character you are inviting into your home: an independe
sassy little terrier, a gentle-mouthed gundog, a sheepc
that will care for the family as it would a flock of sheep
small companion dog that likes to be played with, a c
that is likely to be patient with the quick-fire activities
children, a dog that will warn you of strangers – ev
protect you – a dog that will be quiet, a dog that will
friendly with other dogs, a dog that is unlikely to chew y
furniture or your car. All breeds reflect one o
combination of these characteristics to a greater or les

16

extent, and the degree to which they develop depends substantially on how a puppy is treated, trained and disciplined from the moment you take charge.

Dogs are inherently members of a pack and have the instinctive need to subordinate themselves to their human substitute for a pack leader. The domestication of dogs also means that environment plays a significant role in determining sociability. If a dog has little contact with people it is more likely to be distrustful, aggressive, defensive of food and territory, and difficult to control whatever its breed.

Bear this in mind by taking a little time to identify the sort of companion you and your family will get along with best. Bear in mind, too, that your family circumstances may change during your dog's lifetime. A one-man dog, if not properly socialized at an early age, might object strongly if it had to compete for your affections with the arrival of a partner or a child.

Dog Ownership

HOME AND ENVIRONMENT

Many people have firm views on the rightness or otherwise of keeping a dog inside the house or outside in a suitable pen. Either way, young puppies should start their lives with you inside, and then if it is a hardy breed suited to outdoor life, you can introduce it gradually to its permanent quarters. A dog is a creature of habit, so before you collect your puppy ensure that it has set places to eat, sleep and rest. For ease of cleaning, a kitchen or utility room floor is the best place to put down food and water bowls. The dog's bed, which should be large enough for the adult dog to stretch out in, should be in a draught-free, quiet spot but at the same time not in an area where the dog might feel cut off from the family activities. Some of the shorthaired breeds prefer to be in a warm spot, while longer-haired dogs often prefer a cool place. The furnishings and amount of space you have in your home generally are important factors when you are deciding on the type of dog you want; precious ornaments on low tables, and a favourite but easily marked carpet in your living room do not complement a happy, tail-wagging, soaking wet Labrador.

If you plan to house your dog outdoors, its quarters should be the right size with plenty of room for the dog to stretch out, fully weatherproof and draught free. The pen area should have plenty of well-drained and cleanable

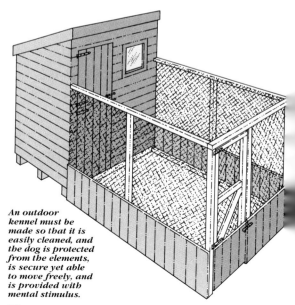

An outdoor kennel must be made so that it is easily cleaned, and the dog is protected from the elements, is secure yet able to move freely, and is provided with mental stimulus.

round with sufficient space for the dog to run about, and the surrounding fence should be of a height and strength to keep the dog in while allowing it to see out and not feel cut off. A dog kept outside needs regular human contact.

Dog owners with easy access to the countryside are fortunate when it comes to exercise. But even they must ensure that they have permission to walk dogs on farmland or in public parks. A healthy dog needs regular exercise and plenty of it. For the city or suburban dweller, therefore, it is essential to check out where you can take your dog in safety. Bear in mind too that cleaning up after your dog is more often than not a legal requirement.

A car is a way of life for many of us, and most dogs enjoy car travel though some do suffer from carsickness and there are pills to combat this. They should travel either on the back seat or in a protected area at the back and not be exposed to draughts, which can cause eye, ear and throat problems. You should carry water and a bowl with you and give the dog drinks at regular intervals especially if the car gets very warm. And, if you are travelling long distances, remember that, like you, your dog will need regular stops to stretch and relieve itself.

There will be times when you have to travel with your dog, if only to the veterinarian or to a dog parlour. And

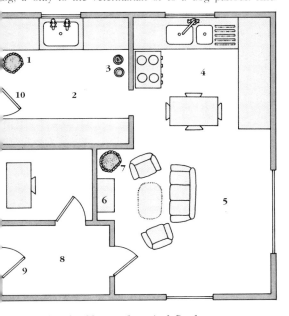

An indoor dog should eat and rest in defined areas. 1 & 7. Dog bed; 2. Utility room; 3. Food/Waterbowls; 4. Kitchen; 5. Living room; 6. Fireplace; 8. Hall; 9 & 10. Exterior doors.

without a car, you may find that public transport wi
present problems. On longer trips, check with bus, air, tra
and taxi services to find out whether you have to use crate
whether your pet can travel with you or in a freight var
and whether you have to provide certificates of vaccinatior
etc. If you are going far afield you may need to "pack
bag" for your dog as well, including such items as
portable bed, special food, bowls, a leash, groomin
equipment, fresh water, and possibly a muzzle. As
yourself, too, whether your dog will be happier travellin
with you or whether it might be happier in a wel
recommended boarding kennel. And if you spend a gre
deal of your time travelling, should you even consid
owning a dog?

The question dog breeders are most often asked
whether the dog they are selling is good with children. I
fact almost all dogs are naturally well disposed towar
children, and some breeds are especially good, while othe
are rather more wary such as some of the smaller bree
that are very owner-orientated. There are always exception
and certainly any dog that is elderly, sick, teased, c
mistreated will become unpredictable. Children must b
taught from babyhood to respect a dog, whether it belong
to the family or a neighbour. A dog is not a human, nc
does it think or behave like one. If it perceives a threat
whether real or imagined – it will react and quickly. Whe
there are small children and a dog in the home, it is onl
sensible to be sure that an adult is keeping an eye o
things. A dog is often seen as a living toy by a child, but
children are encouraged to help with every aspect c
looking after a pet, they soon learn to respect it as a
individual in its own right. However, some of the tin
breeds need to be handled carefully and are not physicall
suited to playing with children.

The arrival of a new baby can also create a problem fc
the dog owner if not handled correctly from the start. Fror
the moment the baby arrives in the house, make sure it
not isolated from the dog. With a well-kept, clean an
worm-free dog, a sniff (though licking should b
discouraged) by way of an introduction is a good idea. Th
dog will soon get the idea that this tiny thing is a new pac
arrival and not an intruder, and sometimes it will becom
quite protective.

Introducing a new puppy to other pets in the househol
has to be done with watchful care and patience. Neve
force the pace. Let them get to know each other in the
own time. An adult dog faced with a new puppy wi
usually accept it quite quickly as long as you make sure th
adult isn't too harassed by puppy pranks and that feedin
times are monitored. It is a sensible idea to feed an adu
separately from a puppy; their mealtimes will be differer
anyway and the adult will not feel threatened. Introducir
grown dogs to each other needs the same watchful care;

20

can take longer for both of them to readjust their pack instincts, and occasionally doesn't work out. There is rarely any problem with puppies and kittens, but a puppy bouncing in on your grown cat's territory usually causes a spat or two with the cat having the upper hand before both settle down quite happily. Your job is to ensure that they don't hurt each other, and that they feel they are still loved as much as before. Other small pets, such as gerbils, hamsters or budgerigars that have had the run of your house will have to be caged when a puppy arrives because it will see them as "prey".

The other important aspect of home and environment for your dog is security. You must ensure that your garden or yard fence is dog proof, that your dog has no access to the public highways unless on a leash under your control, and that it wears a collar and identification tag at all times. Even if your neighbours are dog lovers, they will not relish having their plants dug up or their lawn used as a lavatory. Speak to them before you get your dog, and reassure them that you will take proper care. One of the things that drives neighbours mad, is a dog that barks incessantly. This will occur if you leave a too-dependent dog alone for long periods and do not teach it young enough to relax when left on its own. Don't get a dog if you are going to be out a lot – it isn't fair on the dog nor on your neighbours. If you have a dog-proof yard or garden, then you need not have too many problems with a bitch on heat. But this can be a tiresome time unless you work out a sensible routine from the beginning. During the bleeding phase, the bitch will need to be confined so that the house is not messed up. But at the same time, you must provide a space for her where she can still feel part of daily routine.

COST

Can you afford to have a dog? Think carefully about this, and work it out on paper. A dog's basic requirements are simple, but they are continuous for the whole of its 10 to 15-year lifespan. Note down first the initial outlay including the purchase price of the puppy and essential equipment – bed, bedding, feeding bowls, collars, leash, brush, comb. Then work out the irregular, but essential cost of vaccinations, registration or licence fees (if required) vacation and/or quarantine care, neutering (one-off), insurance, visits to the veterinarian and to the dog parlour.

Then work out what your food bill will amount to on weekly basis; quantity will depend on the type of dog yc want. Costs and prices vary hugely from country to countr and even from area to area or street to street, so chec around your locality to get a reasonably accurate pictur Deduct the one-off costs, divide the irregular costs by 52 ad that to your weekly food bill, and then you will have a approximate idea of what you are adding overall to th household budget each week.

TIME
The life expectancy of a dog varies widely between th breeds and between individuals. A very general rule is tha the larger the dog the shorter its natural lifespan, but 10 t 15 years is what you should anticipate and, of course, muc depends on how fit the dog is. You must be sure that yo not only have the time now, but in years to come as wel to provide your dog with proper exercise – some breec require far more exercise than others – to train and educat it and to continue the education, to play with it and t groom it. These daily activities do take time, but they ar essential, and it is no good discovering that you are unabl to give your dog the time it needs after you have bought i You owe it both to yourself and your pet to be honest.

DISCIPLINE AND TRAINING
It is undoubtedly true that an obedient, well-trainec sociable dog is a delight to be with and is a reflection of th qualities of the dog owner. Simple methods of housetrainin and obedience training are described in more detail later i the book and you should study them carefully befor answering the question whether you have the patience, th self-control, the understanding of a dog's true nature, anc the physical stamina to take your puppy through all th phases of house and toilet training, command training, anc leash training, as well as the other important introduction to social behaviour. Self-discipline in the owner is importar when responding to puppy misdeeds. An over-reaction wil terrify and undermine the learning process. Lessons i obedience and social contact continue throughout a dog'. life, and it is a mistake to think that when your young dog i doing everything you want it to you can relax your vigilance Bad habits can be acquired surprisingly quickly at any age and will persist unless dealt with firmly at the outset.

Obedience classes for dogs are often available locally and some people find them very helpful, but don't be misled into thinking they will supply all the answers. Check them out with other people who have used them before signing on, as sometimes they are geared to training particular types of dog, and a class for German Shepherd: may not be ideal for your King Charles Spaniel. Classes car be particularly useful if your dog has any tendency to be aggressive to other dogs or to people.

THE PROSPECTIVE DOG OWNER'S QUESTIONNAIRE

If you can confidently answer yes to the following, then read through the rest of the chapters in the book before making a decision on what dog is going to be happiest with you and you with it.

1. Do I understand the true nature of a dog?

2. Have I the time, patience and persistence to train my dog properly?

3. Can I afford to
- **buy a dog?**
- **provide the correct diet?**
- **pay veterinary fees?**
- **insure my dog?**
- **pay for care when I am away?**

4. Am I able to
- **look after a dog for the whole of its life?**
- **provide enough space in my home?**
- **provide my dog with a caring environment and plenty of time for daily exercise and play?**
- **ensure my dog will be under my control and supervised at all times in town or country?**
- **clean up after my dog?**
- **ensure my dog will not be a nuisance to neighbours, other members of the public, farm animals and crops, or other people's dogs?**

5. Have I received permission (from a landlord for instance) to keep a dog?

6. Do I know what the law requires of me and my dog?

7. Have I considered objectively my reasons for acquiring a dog?*

*Note:
Take a little time before answering this question. Do you plan to get a dog because your family wants one, or the children are demanding a puppy? Do you feel you need a dog to protect you, or are you simply looking for companionship? You are the one who must want the dog, choose it, and take on all the responsibilities for it. Satisfying the prevailing whim of a child, seeking to enhance your image or to bolster your courage in a mad bad world are not good primary reasons for buying a dog, though they may be the result.

Understanding Your Dog

A dog shows by certain actions what it needs and what it feeling, and its human family needs to recognize thes expressions and to respond to them effectively. They a important factors in successful and happy co-existence.

Studies of wolf pack behaviour in the wild have show clearly how members of the pack subordinate themselves t a pack leader – new leaders only emerging when the o one falters in command – and it is this instinct to accep domination that has made the dog trainable by humans. Th dog owner, just like a pack leader, must of course continu to exercise command throughout the dog's life, recognizin at the same time, however, that factors such as livin conditions, rest and playtime, and social environmen also play a substantial part in raising a well-balanced an well-behaved dog.

COMMUNICATION

A dog will respond to situations through its voice, body and face, though the signals may not be so easy to interpre in dogs with very long hair over their faces, with lon floppy ears, with docked tails and ears, or with tails tha stay naturally between the legs as with Greyhounds.

Vocal range and use varies from breed to breed. Clos observation of your individual dog will soon teach you th meaning of barking, howling, growling, whining, son moaning, and many variations in between that are all par of the repertoire. A bark, for instance, can indicate anythin from a warning to excitement or even boredom. Som dogs hardly bark at all, while others – especially the terrier – tend to make a habit of barking and this needs to b checked early on.

FACIAL AND BODY LANGUAGE

A relaxed dog shows it is contented by a loose posture whether standing, sitting or sprawling on the floor, a gentl gaze, and floppy ears. It responds to gentle words or caress with a gently wagging tail, and if you scratch it in tickly spot it may even wrinkle up its top lip as if grinning roll over on its back and present its vulnerable throat an tummy to be rubbed, or raise a paw as if to shake hands – reflex action going back to puppyhood and "kneading" a its mother's teats. A little more happy excitement and th tail wags vigorously, the body wriggles, and there may b an attempt to lick your face or put both paws up on you knees or shoulders. When discouraging the last two remember that the dog is behaving naturally as it woul when greeting its pack leader, so you need to rechannel it responses by encouraging it to stay down and stepping ou of the way when it jumps up and saying "no" firmly.

A watchful, alert dog is likely to stand up, eyes keen an ears pricked. If it anticipates a happy activity such as a

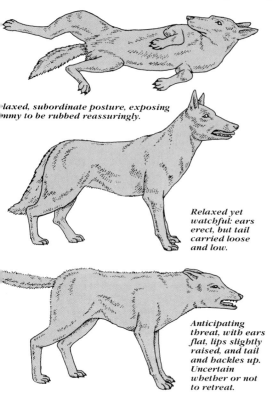

Relaxed, subordinate posture, exposing tummy to be rubbed reassuringly.

Relaxed yet watchful: ears erect, but tail carried loose and low.

Anticipating threat, with ears flat, lips slightly raised, and tail and hackles up. Uncertain whether or not to retreat.

...lk, it wags its tail. However, if it expects a threat, the tail ... still and erect, and the hackles start to stiffen slightly.

A frightened dog cringes, with its tail flattened between ... legs, its lips sometimes slightly raised, its ears flattened, ... its eyes possibly rolling: it doesn't want to be noticed. ...om this posture the dog may run away, or attack. When ...acking, the posture changes very quickly: the ears go ...rward, the hackles go up, the teeth are bared, then as it ...oves in the ears flatten again. Some dogs growl and snarl, ...ile others are virtually silent. Sometimes the aggression is ...ere show and goes no further, at other times the dog will ... straight in. Even with a well trained dog, you need to ...ticipate a potential attack situation and to avoid it.

Anger rising   *Ready to attack*   *Attack*

25

NATURAL DOG BEHAVIOUR

Dogs are naturally sociable creatures, and from a very ear age they should be introduced to as broad a cross-section people and other dogs as possible. When a puppy introduced to a normal adult dog there is unlikely to be a conflict; more often it is a delight to watch the games th ensue. You should remain watchful, however.

When adult dogs meet they go through a pattern behaviour that relates back to their wolf inheritance. The must establish their pack rank. They sniff nose to nose, an check each other anally and then they may ignore ea other, become tail-wagging friends, or stiffen and growl, an if that doesn't resolve rank, move into a fight. Dog fights a usually noisy, but rarely seriously damaging because as soo as one accepts its weaker position it rolls over subordination and the fight ends. It is important, however, understand your own dog's particular character and physic power and to take avoiding action to prevent fights. Son powerfully-jawed and larger breeds can inflict damage ve quickly, and some of the more tenacious terriers seem

believe they a Rottweilers. A d on a leash has greater self-confi ence and is mo likely to initiate fight than whe off it, but the de owner has mo immediate contr Dog owners shou not feel ashame of using muzzle on any dog th has the ability inflict damage. The dogs quickly adapt to them, and they o not restrict a dog's full enjoyment of walks. The more yo encourage your dog to be sociable with other dogs, th happier and better behaved it will be.

Male dogs have a natural instinct to mark out the territory, and this they do by cocking their leg to urina and to leave their scent. So give them time to sniff out oth scents on walks and deposit their own. A fully house-traine dog may do this when in a new house, particularly if the are other dogs around. Correction should be instant, but is nevertheless only doing what is natural. Bitches are n normally territorial, they squat to urinate and do not both much with sniffing unless they are close to, or on, heat.

All dogs have very acute senses of smell, taste, sigh touch and hearing, and some of the senses are developed a fine degree in certain breeds. A dog knows where it is l scent, it has excellent night vision and can perceiv movement at more than twice the range of a human, an

can hear sounds that are inaudible to us. It also has a very sensitive nose, tongue, whiskers and foot pads. This level of sensitivity gives the dog owner great advantages in training but care has to be taken not to abuse these natural assets.

Other behavioural patterns in dogs that relate back to their wild ancestral heritage are burying and digging for food (which you will need to discourage if you are a keen gardener) and scratching out sleeping holes, which they may do outside if they spend a lot of time out in the yard or garden, or try to do to your floor and to their bedding. The turning round before going to sleep is merely its way of getting into the right position and shape to protect its more vulnerable parts from the elements.

NATURAL GROWTH PHASES

The importance of understanding the basic stages of a dog's growth from newborn puppy to adult at about eight months cannot be underestimated in training.

The puppy is born blind and deaf with an instinct only to reach its mother's teats and to suckle. By three weeks it will be pottering about a little, and from four to six weeks it is increasingly discovering the world around: playing, mock fighting, competing for food and finding its place in the litter. This is an important time for plenty of human contact and handling, and good breeders will ensure puppies receive this care and attention.

In the third month the learning curve accelerates. The puppy learns just how far it can go with its parent and its brothers and sisters and how to use its strength to full advantage. This is the period in which a puppy will go to its new human owner and play training can begin immediately. During the three and four-month stage the owner and the rest of the human household should fully establish positions as pack leader and superior pack members. Housetraining and simple commands should be understood; games and play as well as controlled periods of undisturbed rest can be used to encourage self-confidence and self-awareness; and social contacts should be broadened beyond the household environs. In the fifth and sixth months the puppy, if it were a wolf cub, would start to be taken out with the pack to learn hunting. The domestic pet will likewise look for ways to broaden its horizons, so training patterns should be established. Now is the time to introduce your puppy to experiences such as busy roads, noise and bustle and

27

encourage it to be perfectly confident in a variety of situations. From the seventh to eighth months the puppy moves swiftly through adolescence when it will try to make its own rules unless the owner retains dominance with continuous contact, consistency and firm correction. The bonds of friendship, loyalty and obedience should be well cemented by adulthood at eight months.

ABNORMAL DOG BEHAVIOUR

Character and behaviour defects are usually the result of genetic faults inherited through poor breeding, human mishandling during the impressionable puppy and early adult stages, or brain damage caused by disease.

A disturbed or anti-social dog can be very difficult to cure, and in many instances will have to be destroyed. Unprovoked and excessive aggression and biting are extremely serious problems, and perhaps the most common. They can also be the result of insufficient early social contact with other people and other dogs, and even through misguidedly treating a dog as a human. Neutering can sometimes alleviate the problem in male dogs, but only when allied to a long and consistent programme of muzzled reintroduction to a wide range of dogs and people, and firm and fast correction whenever aggression is displayed. Dog behaviour and training classes can be useful as a controlled environment in which to reintroduce the dog to society. But, not all such classes accept over-aggressive animals.

Over-sensitive or highly neurotic dogs are equally difficult to deal with. Loud noises and sudden actions will startle even a well-balanced dog, but they can reduce an over-sensitive dog to a quivering wreck with inconsistent and unnatural responses. Extreme patience and gentle but firm handling combined with very gradual reintroductions to the varying stimuli may sometimes help. But you cannot force the pace if self-confidence is to build up. The root causes of terror reactions may never come to light, but one of the most common is ill-treatment of a young puppy or young dog, and some breeds, or some overbred individuals, will remain highly sensitive all their lives.

Excessive destructiveness to objects such as furniture, carpets, and doors can be caused by bad environmental conditions during the dog's early months. When puppies are losing their milk teeth and growing their adult teeth they need to chew. If they are not provided with their own chewable "toys", they will naturally munch on anything within reach. Lack of proper food, exercise, and companionship inevitably leads to boredom and frustration. Keeping the dog in regular loving contact with you and others helps to break the pattern of destructiveness, but the owner still needs to remain firm and consistent, and the dog should learn to relax and rest quietly for reasonable periods of time on its own.

Buying a Dog

The golden rule is *NEVER* buy a dog or puppy on impulse. Having decided whether you want an adult dog or a puppy, a particular breed, a crossbreed or a mongrel, a dog or a bitch, allow yourself plenty of time to check out fully where you are going to buy it from. Breed societies will supply information about breeders and may also have adult dogs of a particular breed left with them by previous owners for good or bad reasons. Registered breeders do not always have puppies available, and the good breeders of popular dogs often have waiting lists for the next litter, so be prepared to wait too. You may have friends who have bred from their pet bitch or are about to do so, and you may particularly want a dog like theirs. You may want to give a good home to an abandoned puppy or dog from your local animal shelter. You may feel you can do it the easy way and order a puppy by mail order, through an agent or from your local pet shop. These last three options should be avoided because you have no way of finding out about breeding history and conditions, or the health of the dog or puppy.

BUYING FROM A BREEDER

There are good breeders, there are unscrupulous breeders, and there are puppy farms. These farms go in for mass production of pedigree puppies, usually of several breeds, simply to make as much money as possible. The animals survive in minimal conditions, and the puppies' physical and mental health is often permanently damaged. You can only be certain you have found a good breeder, if, after it has been recommended to you, you personally check the kennels. You should see the bitch and check her credentials, check the credentials of the sire too and check back on the breeding lines of both. Check also the kennel conditions and what deworming and vaccination proof will be supplied when you collect your puppy. Advise the owners that you will have your puppy checked by your veterinarian within 48 hours of your acquiring it. A reputable breeder will expect you to be satisfied on all these counts and will in turn want to question you on how well you are prepared for the puppy. You should visit the litter and choose your puppy at about six weeks old when it should be friendly, curious and alert. (An obviously timid pup could be mentally impaired.) A good breeder will recognize different points in each individual puppy, and should advise you on what to look for if you are in any doubt. Eight to ten weeks is the best age to get your puppy as by then it will be weaned and eating solids. (Some breeders may keep them for longer.) When you collect your puppy ask for advice on the specific diet it has been having and keep to this initially when you take it home. Most reputable breeders will supply a diet sheet for you to follow they will be as concerned as you that your puppy settles

quickly and happily in its new home. The pedigree cha
showing the purebreed ancestry of your pup, and th
certificates of vaccination should be handed over to you
the same time.

BUYING PRIVATELY
Private breeders, or friends and acquaintances may own
bitch that you particularly like and that is going to have
litter. This may be the result of an organized mating with
dog of the same breed, or another purebreed, or a
accidental mating. The bitch herself may not be a pedigre
dog, but a lovely affectionate creature just the sam
Whatever the puppies' ancestry, it is worthwhile knowing
much as you can about it so that you can make an educate
guess how your puppy will turn out. Much of the advic
that applies to buying a puppy from a registered breed
applies here too: the signs to look for when selecting yo
puppy at six weeks, the age at which to take it home, th
following of the same diet. All puppies have the right to
good start in life, and you have the right to know that yo
puppy comes to you fully fit and ready.

BUYING FROM ANIMAL RESCUE CENTRES
It is perhaps a sad reflection on our society that anim
shelters and rescue homes will normally be able to provid
a wide variety of dogs to choose from: puppies, youn
dogs, dogs of several years, very small dogs, very larg
dogs, bitches and males, mongrels and pedigree dog
(Many breed societies run rescue centres for specific bree
and they can be traced through central directories availab
from national kennel clubs.) Sometimes, the shelter will b
able to provide some background history on individu
dogs but more often you will have to rely on your ow
observations. There is a risk, of course. You will have n
clear guidelines on inherited character traits, and ofte
particularly with the older dogs, you won't know wheth
there are emotional scars left over from its unknown ear
months. Any dog that is obviously abnormal or showin
signs of aberrant behaviour will not or should not be sol
But normally the dogs are so happy to be away from th
inevitable restrictions of a shelter, that they will respon
quickly and well to the individual attention and trainin
they receive from their new owner and make delightf
companions and pets. When collecting a dog from such
centre, make sure it has been fully checked medically, an
vaccinated. Sometimes, the centres demand that the dog
bitch is neutered either by themselves or by you. This is
wise policy. They may also insist on implanting a
identification tag, which is a small operation by injectio
and does not impair the dog in anyway. Some countri
insist on this by law for all dogs – working dogs, pedigre
dogs, and mongresl – to assist with tracing ownership whe
abandoned or stray dogs are found.

PRICE

A new dog or puppy buyer should expect to pay more or less than their puppy is worth. Even a mongrel puppy is worth at least the cost of its keep and veterinary care during the first eight to ten weeks of its life. The price of a pedigree dog from a registered breeder is quoted to you when you confirm your selection of your puppy, and should reflect whether you are buying a pet or show quality dog. And when you choose a dog from a rescue centre, the fee may include a contribution to the charity as well as the cost of the individual dog.

The appeal of young puppies is hard to resist, particularly when you instinctively want to "save" them. However, the high failure rate in puppy viability and dog/owner relationships is so often the result of an impulse purchase.

Care and Training

DIET

The nutritional requirements for dogs have been clos[e]
studied by scientists, and essentially they retain the sa[me]
proportions of carbohydrates, fats, proteins, vitamins a[nd]
minerals that make up the natural diet of wolves. Dogs [are]
omnivores and will eat a wide range of foods, and provid[ed]
dog owners ensure that they are providing the right bala[nce]
at the right time, they can select the diet best suited [to]
themselves and their dog. The quantity and the quality [of]
the food given to a dog is determined by its size a[nd]
normal weight, the amount of exercise it takes, and its a[ge.]
Young puppies, pregnant and lactating bitches, do[gs]
recovering from illness, seriously underweight [or]
overweight dogs, and older dogs may require diet[ary]
supplements, but these should only be supplied [on]
veterinary advice. Broadly speaking, however, the food y[ou]
provide for your eight- to ten-week old puppy will cont[ain]
the same balance as you give to your dog all its life. Y[ou]
must ensure it receives the correct proportions of calciu[m,]
phosphorous and vitamin D for bone growth and gene[ral]
development, and high quality protein – eggs and da[iry]
products are recommended – but essentially only [the]
quantity, timing and number of meals will vary.

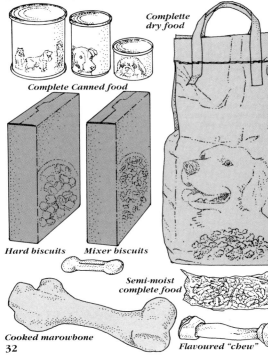

Complette dry food

Complete Canned food

Hard biscuits *Mixer biscuits*

Semi-moist complete food

Cooked marrowbone

Flavoured "chew"

arbobydrates normally make up to about 40 to 50 percent of the daily intake of an adult dog, but down to 25 percent for growing dogs. They supply bulk, fibre and provide energy for daily activity. Common sources of carbohydrates are cereals and grains (rice must be cooked), potatoes (also cooked), biscuits and bread.

ats provide energy and flavour, and often supply the texture of the dog's meal. The amount of fat provided should not be less than ten percent and can go up as high as 30 percent. All meats supply fat as does sunflower oil, etc. Fat deficiency can cause dry skin and lower resistance to disease.

rotein is broken down in the digestive system into essential amino acids for normal growth and the maintenance of metabolism. Both the quality and quantity of the protein provided are extremely important in ensuring the health of your dog. A daily intake of at least 12 percent high quality protein is essential, and the average is about 18 percent and higher for growing dogs and dogs that do much physical work. Meat, eggs, and fish are high in protein as are pulses such as peas and soya, cheese and some cereals.

ssential minerals and vitamins are naturally provided in cereals and vegetables.

Unlike humans, dogs thrive on an unchanging diet. This is why it is so important with young puppies that no dramatic change is made to either the content or timing of their meals when you first take them home. Changes should be made gradually, until you end up feeding one or two meals a day using the range of food that your dog enjoys and you find easiest to supply whether at home or travelling. It is not uncommon for puppies and grown dogs to bolt their food. This can cause indigestion or, more seriously, gastric torsion (see page 137). It is sensible to monitor the speed of intake particularly after exercise.

Convenience foods for dogs are big business, and it should not be surprising that this is so. Quality products – and you must check labels for nutritional balance and content – are usually palatable for the dogs and easy to buy, store and provide. Canned food, semi-moist or semi-dry food, and dry food are all available and can be used on their own or mixed with proprietory mixers, your own scraps, etc.

Water, freshly supplied every day, must always be available to your dog. The amount drunk varies from dog to dog, and depends on the sort of food you supply, amount of exercise, and climate.

Dogs are natural scavengers, so you should avoid putting temptation in their way and teach them at an early age to eat only the food you give them. There are many treats and titbits you can buy for a dog, and these are useful aids while training. But remember to allow for them in their overall daily intake and avoid sweets.

There has always been a debate on whether it is better to cook fresh meat or to supply it raw. The risk of supplying infected meat to your dog is obviously considerably reduced if it is thoroughly cooked. Most dogs love chewing on bones. The only bones that are safe for your dog are large shin bones, preferably cooked. Avoid bones that splinter easily or could even remotely be swallowed whole. You can buy bone substitutes, and these can be particularly useful for puppies when they are teething. Dry biscuits are helpful to control any tartar build-up on teeth.

As dogs get older, they naturally eat less and, while the quality of the protein may be increased, the overall balance remains constant, and quantity may be reduced gradually by about ten percent.

Certain breeds are more likely to run to fat, but owners are largely responsible for the high percentage of pet dogs that are overweight: too much food, too many treats, over rich diets, insufficient exercise. If you really care for your dog's health, avoid overfeeding. Obesity can lead to problems for dogs just as it can for humans: difficulties with breathing, heart failure, liver, excema and diabetes are just a few. But if your dog show signs of being overweight, then consult your veterinarian who will advise you on how to gradually introduce your dog to a safe reducing diet and then how to maintain the right weight for its size and lifestyle. You should also ask your veterinarian for advice on special diets or food supplements for a dog that is recovering from illness, or for a bitch that is pregnant or suckling puppies.

The following charts provide guidelines only on average daily quantities and timing of meals for puppies, growing dogs and adults. Each breed of dog varies slightly in its needs, and the lifestyle you provide for your dog will also affect the timing and levels of food it requires.

CALORIE/KILOJOULE GUIDE

The energy needs of your dog can be worked out by using kilojoules or calories as your measure. Balanced proprietary brands of dog foods should indicate quantities on their labels for a range of dog sizes. If you are making the meals yourself, you need to balance the percentage of nutritional elements to the correct quantity and bulk for the size of your dog.

Canned foods can be mixed with mixer biscuits to increase bulk. Semi-moist/dry, and dry dog foods contain less water and have a higher calorie content.

100g (4oz) High protein canned dog food = 380Kj (90c)
100g (4oz) Complete semi-moist/dry food = 1,340Kj (320c)

DULT DOG CHART

MATURE DOG SIZE/ WEIGHT	DAILY KILOJOULE/ CALORIE REQUIREMENT	TYPE OF FOOD	QUANTITY/ WEIGHT
mall dogs p to 4.5kg 10lb)	1,000–2,000Kj 240–480c	Dry Semi-moist Canned Made-up	55–115g (2–4oz) 115–125g (4–4½oz) ¼–½ tin 250–600g (½–1¼lb)
mall- ledium ogs .5–9kg 10–20lb)	2,000–3,000Kj 480–720c	Dry Semi-moist Canned Made-up	115–200g (4–7oz) 125–225g (4½–8oz) ½–1 tin 600–1,250g (1¼–2½lb)
ledium ogs -14kg 20–30lb)	3,000–4,000Kj 720–960c	Dry Semi-moist Canned Made-up	200–300g (7–10oz) 225–335g (8–12oz) 1–1¼ tins 1,250–1,700g (1¼–3¾lb)
ledium- arge dogs 4-22kg 30-50lb)	4,000–6,000Kj 960–1,430c	Dry Semi-moist Canned Made-up	300–400g (10–14oz) 335–450g (12oz–1lb) 1¼–1½ tins 1,700–2,480g (3¾–5½lb)
arge dogs 2–34kg 50–75lb)	6,000–8,000Kj 1,430–1,900c	Dry Semi-moist Canned Made-up	400–525g (14–18oz) 450–600g (1–1¼lb) 1½–2½ tins 2,480–3,400g (5½–7½lb)
'ery large logs 4–80kg 75-170lb)	8,000–14,000Kj 1,900–3,300c	Dry Semi-moist Canned Made-up	525–820g (18oz–1¾lb) 600–900g (1¼–2lb) 2½–3½ tins 3,400–3,530 (7½–7¾lb)

otes:

- The smaller the dog the more energy it will use daily.
- Small dogs mature up to a year earlier than large dogs.
- Approximate conversions have been used throughout.
- A standard can of dog food has been calculated as weighing 400g (14oz). Bulk is added to canned food using mixer biscuits to manufacturer's recommendations, or how best suits the individual dog.

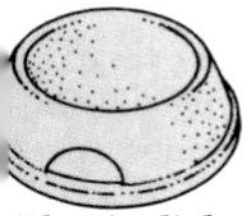

Plastic dish

Stainless steel dish

Pottery dish

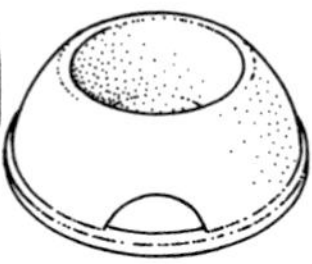

Raised bowl

PUPPY CHART
(Daily requirements for a puppy that will grow into a
14kg (30lb) adult dog.)

Age	Kilojoules	Calories
2 - 2½ months	2,600 - 3,200	620 - 760
2½ - 3 months	3,200 - 4,000	760 - 950
3 - 4 months	4,000 - 4,600	950 - 1,095
4 - 5 months	4,600 - 5,600	1,095 - 1,340
5 - 6 months	5,600	1,340
6 months upwards	Gradually reduce over the next year to:	
	4,000	950

Note:
As a rough guide, divide by two for small dogs and
multiply by two or more for large dogs. Most breeders
will supply a feeding chart for your puppy, and
reputable proprietary brands make special high protein
foods for puppies and growing dogs.

DAILY CARE
The routine of caring for your dog begins from the moment
you acquire it. You will have established beforehand the
feeding area with suitable bowls for food and water, and
dog bed of the correct size will be in a draught-free, central
position so that even the smallest puppy will be
comfortable and relaxed in it whenever it is not doing
things with you. Dogs are happiest if their lives follow
reasonably regular routine, and so it is important to
establish your patterns of daily care from day one.

Grooming Handle a puppy gently but firmly to begin with
to acquaint it with the procedures. If handled correctly at
the start, your dog will soon enjoy being groomed. The coat
of the dog determines the equipment you will need: a hand
mitten or chamois leather, a fine comb and a bristle brush
for short coats; a wire brush, an open-toothed comb, and
depending on the fineness of the coat, a firm bristle brush for
rough and long coats. Start by feeling through the coat to
the skin with your fingers and remove anything caught up
in the hair, and then groom going with the lie of the coat,
finishing with the brush or leather for shorthaired dogs, and
with the comb for longhaired and rough-coated dogs,
brushing the hair both ways beforehand. All longhaired
dogs should be groomed every day.

Handstripping, or pinching out fur, is simple to do on
small dogs where the undercoat comes away easily.
Heavier-coated dogs are better dealt with by trained hands.
Trimming or stripping knives and combs are good for
shortening dense coats, and scissors are essential for
trimming the ever-growing curls of Poodles.

MEALS

Age	No of Meals
2 - 3 months	4
3 - 4 months	3
4 - 9 months	2
9 - 12 months	2
1 - 2 years	1 or 2

Notes:
1. At two months puppies should be fully weaned.
2. Mealtimes should be evenly spaced.
3. Changes to mealtimes should be gradually introduced.
4. Allow one hour relaxation before and after meals.
5. Large dogs mature more slowly than small dogs. Toys mature at around one year, very large dogs at around two years.

Grooming equipment

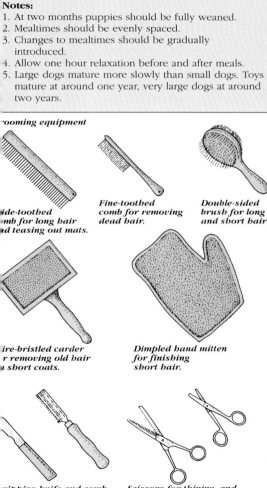

Wide-toothed comb for long hair and teasing out mats.

Fine-toothed comb for removing dead hair.

Double-sided brush for long and short hair

Wire-bristled carder for removing old hair in short coats.

Dimpled hand mitten for finishing short hair.

Stripping knife and comb for removing dead hair and shortening coat.

Scissors for thinning, and scissors for trimming (blunt-ended).

Baths Only bath your dog if it cannot be cleaned ▮ grooming. Puppies should only be bathed if absolute necessary and following veterinary advice on bo procedure and shampoo, and adult dogs preferably n more than twice a year and again using good quali shampoos and conditioners formulated to avoid upsetti the natural oil balance of skin and coat.

Tepid water can be used to rinse off excess mud aft wet walks, followed by a good rub down with a towel that the dog does not stay wet for longer than necessar Water never hurt any dog and some, like the retrievers, lo it, but do not start adding shampoo unless you have to ar then use one specially prepared for dogs.

Many breeds with long or rough coats benefit fro trimming or stripping particularly in summer, and this al makes them easier to groom. You can use a pair of clippi shears yourself for a rough clip, but you will need special help from your local pet parlour for more exotic clips or f hand-stripping.

Exercise Different breeds need varying amounts of exercis but almost all must be exercised energetically eve day to keep fully fit. A walk on the leash is not sufficier but a good time spent in romping play will help kee muscles in trim. Retrieving balls is a game which usua▮ tires the owner long before the dog wants to stop. Ar where only limited exercise is available outdoors, a dog ca have a lot of fun playing with its own toys insid particularly if you join in. Well-organized games will hel keep a dog mentally and physically alert and are importar in training regimes.

Eyes, ears, feet and teeth Remove any natural discharge from the eyes with a clean, damp cloth or damp cotto wool when they appear, but if any other symptoms ar manifest consult a veterinarian. Check ears regularly for di wax build up, and parasites, and clean once a month with lightly oiled pad, though do not probe into the sensitiv inner channels. Some breeds have hair growing right dow in the ear canal which causes the wax to build up and m and not flow out naturally, such ears are much mor difficult to keep clean, but you can pinch out, or carefull clip away any visible waxy lumps of hair with blunt-ende scissors. Long-eared dogs are more prone to ear problem but any dog that is shaking its head a lot or scratching i ears should be taken to a veterinarian. Check feet, pads an nails regularly. Keep hair between the pads of longhaire dogs trimmed – not too short – to avoid balls of mud (snow developing, and a pad massage with a little petroleu jelly can help minor wounds or cracking. Overlong nail should be trimmed by a professional. Teeth scaling is also job for professionals but your dog should not suffer teeth (gum problems if properly fed with crunchy food, or, if it i

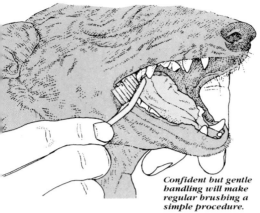

Confident but gentle handling will make regular brushing a simple procedure.

rone to tartar build up, use a canine toothpaste and brush s teeth regularly. The earlier teeth brushing is begun, the nore easily the dog will adapt to the procedure.

Communication Dogs are very sociable creatures and espond quickly to voice and actions. They need to be egularly reassured by your presence, a word of praise or orrection, a pat or caress on the back or head and a little hat now and then. By doing this you reassert your status as lpha dog or pack leader and they remain a happy member f the pack.

TRAINING YOUR DOG

Wild dogs live in packs in which unpacklike behaviour is lealt with immediately by senior dogs or the alpha dog and s simply not tolerated. In the case of your dog the same ule applies, which is why it is so important not to leave uppies unsupervised or free to range around your home nd garden before they understand your rules of good ehaviour.

The most important learning phase in a puppy's life is rom eight to 12 weeks. Bad habits acquired at this time are lifficult to eradicate later, while responses to command and ood behaviour, if consistently encouraged, will remain a olid foundation on which to build a harmonious elationship. You need to be there to say a firm "no" vhenever a misdemeanour is committed. And it is no good hastising a dog minutes or hours later, it must be done at he time. If "no" does not work, throw something at the dog - not anything that will hurt it or your furniture but omething that will startle it – and reinforce your action by nother sharp "no". Smacking and beating or inflicting any ind of physical pain is useless and can seriously impair sychological development.

The earliest commands a puppy has to learn are "no" and come", and, of course its name. A bright young puppy will

A puppy will "come" in expectation of praise or a treat. But, when learning to "stay", you will train it to come only when you give the command.

want to come to you naturally, and you can build on this by saying "come" encouragingly and then rewarding it with a dog biscuit as a treat or with plenty of praise. Don't give titbit every time, just often enough so that the puppy will respond to your call in expectation; but you must always be lavish in your praise. It is a good idea to carry a few biscuit around with you wherever you go with your dog.

So, the basic guidelines for the new dog owner are: being there, particularly in the early months, most of the time simple training from the moment the puppy arrives establishing the rules for your dog right at the start and the sticking to them; maintaining at all times your position a pack leader or alpha dog; building on the dog's natural instinct to please you; training your dog to do what you want by reward and encouragement and preventing it from doing what you do not want by sharp reprimand.

HOUSETRAINING

A puppy should not be made to feel guilty about relieving itself. When you first bring it into your home you must expect it to leave puddles whenever it has the need, for that is exactly what it will have been doing before. If you do not want puddle stains on your best carpet, you must restrict your puppy to certain areas until it learns to go where you want it to go.

You need to watch it very carefully at first to recognize when it wants to empty its bladder or bowels, and then take it outside, preferably to the same spot, praising it when it responds correctly. Anticipating the time accurately is the key. If you follow a routine of taking it out first thing in the morning, whenever it has eaten or drunk, after it has been sleeping, and last thing at night and praising it when it does what it should where it should, the puppy will soon learn what is expected and tell you it wants to go out. Night housetraining takes longer, because a pup will not naturally contain itself for as long as eight hours. However, by five or six months your puppy should be fully housetrained.

Some breeds, a few of the terriers for instance, do appear to take longer than others; and some bitches do have bladder problems caused by an anatomical fault or general weakness sometimes exacerbated by obesity or old age which can often be alleviated with intermittent and small doses of female hormones. "Emotional bladder syndrome" is not an uncommon problem where an over-excited dog or bitch puddles uncontrollably often when greeting its human family. One answer is to try to ensure the greeting ritual occurs outside; another is to avoid making too much fuss of the dog and keeping your greeting to a few gentle words until it learns to control its excitement.

People with limited outside access can use exactly the same methods to housetrain puppies to relieve themselves in a particular area on newspaper or litter. However, while indoor facilities will work adequately for small dogs and as a temporary measure for puppies, after the age of about six months males will start to cock their legs.

City dwellers also have a responsibility to ensure their dogs do not foul footpaths, whether in parks or on the sidewalks. Right from the start the puppy should be encouraged to use the gutter, and where this is not possible it is your duty to remove the faeces to a suitable bin. Make sure you carry with you a roll of paper towel, a plastic bag, throw-away plastic gloves to protect your hands, or a special scoop that can be purchased at most good pet stores. The best ones are double-handled and spring loaded to pick up material cleanly in a piece of paper towel.

OBEDIENCE TRAINING

A well-trained dog is housetrained, responds to its name, and to the basic commands – "come", "lie down", "sit", "stay" and "no" – walk to heel on or off the leash, can withstand distractions and obeys you in your home, in other people's homes, in public places, and when travelling. It is the irresponsible dog owner who allows a dog to bark uncontrollably, bounce around overexcitedly or chase other animals – natural behaviour to the dog but inappropriate in a human environment.

A normally intelligent dog should be able to understand and respond to more than 20 words of command, and individual owners will use their own. The following basic training guide is simply what all dogs whatever their breed should be taught.

Your dog will soon learn from the tone of your voice how you want it to respond, so you must be consistent in both the commands you regularly use and the tone of your voice when you use them.

Leash training Give your puppy time to get used to wearing a collar. It should be light at first and loose enough not to give too much pressure on the neck, yet tight enough not to pull off over the ears. Collars should be checked and

adjusted regularly on growing dogs. Once it is used to th
collar, gently lead the puppy around in the house with th
leash attached. It will resist at first, but will soon get used
the leash as long as you do not try to drag it. You can no
start to take your dog for walks outside. It will be a b
nervous at first, so you need to reassure it with your voi
and encourage it to stay close to you. As it gains
confidence you need to firmly insist that it walks to "heel".

Dogs that live in a town environment rarely have th
opportunity to run loose, but you can give them additio
freedom by using an extending leash. However, the
should never be any confusion in the dog's mind abo
when it is walking close to you, to heel, and when it ca
run loose whether on an extending leash or off it. Wheth
on a long or short leash, the dog must never be allowed
pull. This is particularly important with strong heavy dog
but is true for all. An alternative training "collar", known
a Halti, is available in some countries and this works by
slip over the jaw. It puts no pressure on the dog's neck, b
if the dog pulls away its head is pulled round by
tightening over the muzzle, and it quickly stops pulling.

Walking to heel "Heel" is a command that should b
obeyed instantly. The training begins with walking on
leash, and is best done in your garden or yard or in a qui
spot with no distractions. Start with only short sessions an

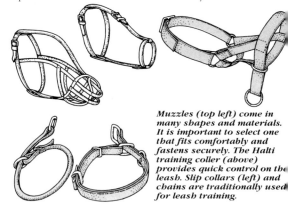

*Muzzles (top left) come in
many shapes and materials.
It is important to select one
that fits comfortably and
fastens securely. The Halti
training collar (above)
provides quick control on the
leash. Slip collars (left) and
chains are traditionally used
for leash training.*

plenty of play and games in between, so your dog does n
get bored and sees the training as part of a game
Traditionally a dog is kept at heel on your left, but it doe
not really matter which side as long as you are consisten
Keep the dog on a short leash, not tight, and walk on. A
the dog begins to go ahead, give it a sharp pull back, sayin
"heel" firmly at the same time, and then relax the leas
Repeat the procedure until your dog stays at heel for a
long as you require after you give a single command. Som
people find it helpful to have a cardboard tube or roll o

newspaper carried in front of the dog's head – not to hit it with, but to show where it should be walking. Once you have leash-trained your dog to walk to heel, repeat the training without the leash using only the tone of your voice as the restraint. After every training session you must reward your dog with plenty of praise and a game or two. Heel training never really ends, but you should feel quite confident that your dog can resist all distraction before you take it into a public place without a leash, so walk it in places where it will experience traffic, other dogs, cats and children, etc. and keep it on a leash until it is fully responsive to the basic commands.

"Come", "Sit", "Lie down", "Stay" These four commands are the essential vocabulary for good behaviour. They should start to be applied from the earliest moments. It is enormously satisfying to train a willing dog, and can be fun, too, both for you and your dog, particularly when incorporated in games in the early days. The tone of your voice, not the words, will be what the dog understands, so use a different tone for each and remain consistent. "Come" can be used with a whistle – if you can whistle – and your dog's name. Always have a treat to hand, particularly to begin with, and always reward a correct response with lavish praise. Practise inside and outside, whenever the opportunity arises and your dog will quickly come for its reward. And if your dog does not respond instantly, then ignore it. Do not punish it or it will become less anxious to please you.

"Sit" is taught by saying the word at the same time as pressing the dog down on its hindquarters until it is sitting, and then praising and rewarding it. Use the same technique for "lie down", but you will have to use both hands. While repeating the command, push down with one hand on the hindquarters and then, as soon as your dog is sitting push the forelegs forward with the other hand until the dog is lying down. Hold the dog in position while you praise it. Both "sit" and "lie down" should be taught at the same time as "stay". But, "stay" is a command that your dog has to learn to obey in any situation – close to you or quite far away. You want it to stop in whatever place or position it is in and stay there, and only to move to you when you command "come". You can practise this command in your home or in your garden or yard, but not in a public place until you are confident your dog will obey you instantly. Place your dog in one position, say "stay" firmly and then move away. As soon as the dog moves, return it to its position and start again. Move away only a short distance to begin with and then further, into another room or out of sight, as the dog learns to stay longer. End each practice with the command "come" and lavish praise and titbits when your dog bounces over to you. This command must be obeyed when you are in other houses, in public places, or need to stop your dog from running off.

Other commands your dog should learn are "leave" or "let go" – best learnt during retrieving games with balls when you take the ball out of its mouth and say the word. Dogs can be very possessive over toys, food and bones, and must learn to "leave" them whenever you say the word, and you must praise them when they do.

Obedience classes These classes for training dogs are popular and successful in some areas, and non-existent in others. They can be helpful to dog owners with no previous experience in dog training, and marginally helpful to the dogs, but full obedience depends on continuity and consistency from owners. They also help to encourage sociability between the different dogs. But check them out first as some are geared to training specific types of dog.

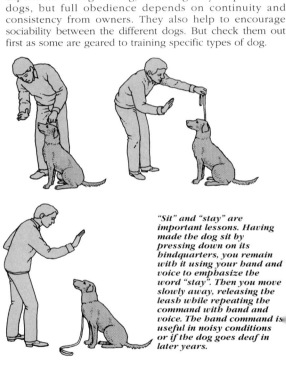

"Sit" and "stay" are important lessons. Having made the dog sit by pressing down on its hindquarters, you remain with it using your hand and voice to emphasize the word "stay". Then you move slowly away, releasing the leash while repeating the command with hand and voice. The hand command is useful in noisy conditions or if the dog goes deaf in later years.

Illustrated Guide to Dogs

The breeds included here represent those dogs that are popular as pets and those that are of interest because of their breeding history and use. So, for instance, while there are many national varieties of hounds, we include only those more commonly available to the general public.

Most of the breeds illustrated are those popular in America and Britain, but we also include breeds from France, Germany, Belgium, Holland, Italy, Scandinavia, Russia, Japan, Tibet, Australia, and elsewhere, that have achieved international interest.

The dogs are presented in groups that are understood internationally, keeping like with like as far as possible. Individual countries have their own systems, but the groups are easy to identify, and where a breed is known by a different names in English, all the names are included. All the breeds illustrated are listed in the index at the end of the book. The illustrations are not drawn to scale, so appearance should be viewed together with caption information on height and weight. The groups are: gundogs, hounds, working (herding) dogs, other working and utility dogs (non-herding), terriers, Spitz or Nordic dogs, and toy dogs. This system was used by Ferelith Somerfield in her *World Encyclopaedia of Dogs* and combines the British "non-sporting" group with "other working and utility dogs".

The captions in this section are extremely brief. They provide succint information on history, appearance, qualities as a pet and temperament. Average heights and weights are also shown, ranging from lighter bitches to heavier dogs, but when buying a pet these details are not so vital as the health and viability of the animal itself. Certain terms are used to describe anatomical features, two of which may need explanation. The *stop* is where the forehead drops from the eyes to the start of the nose, and the *occiput* is the top, back part of the skull.

To the first time buyer of a pedigree dog we cannot emphasize too strongly the importance of researching very carefully the credentials of breeders and their breeding lines. This can be done by personal recommendations, through breed societies, through veterinarians and through taking up references with other owners of dogs from the same stock and breeder.

Finally, a note on aggression. Proper socialization with other animals and people, and consistent correction in puppyhood and training will help to control such behaviour. However, some irresponsible and unscrupulous breeders do breed from unfit animals with over-aggressive temperaments to produce dogs for the "macho" market. So, anyone seeking a family pet from any of the guard breeds should make sure they buy from stock where over-aggressiveness has been bred out and not in.

Gundogs

POINTER/ENGLISH POINTER

History Refined to its present standard in Britain at the end of the 19th century, this aristocrat is said to contain Italian Pointer, Foxhound, Bull Terrier, Greyhound, Newfoundland, Setter and Bulldog amongst its ancestors.

Appearance Superbly proportioned, well-muscled, it has a distinctive dish face with deep, broad forehead. Ears, hang close and straight; eyes, soft hazel or chestnut; tail, straight and tapering. On the point, its rigidly held pose is remarkable.

Height: 54-60cm (20-24in).
Weight: 25kg (55lb).
Coat: fine and short.
Colour: black and white, liver and white, lemon and white, all black and tricolour.
Characteristics Essentially a working dog, intelligent and kindly, it is a good family dog requiring light grooming, and a great deal of working exercise.

GERMAN SHORTHAIRED POINTER/KURZHAAR

History An old German breed, developed from Bloodhound, Spanish and German Pointers amongst others and more recently the Pointer, this is a fine multi-purpose sporting dog.

Appearance Typified by a solid, clean outline overall it has a broad slightly long head. Ears, hang close; eyes, light to dark brown; tail, straight, often docked.

Height: 53-64cm (21-25in).
Weight: 21-32kg (45-70lb).
Coat: flat, short and coarse.
Colour: variations of white with black, chestnut or liver, or roan or solid liver or black.
Characteristics Hardy, intelligent, equable natured with children, it can be trained as a guard dog. Requires moderate grooming, and plenty of hard exercise.

46

ﾍUVERGNE POINTER/BRAQUE D'AUVERGNE

ﾍstory Most likely developed from the Gascony Pointer and the
ｬ Pyrenean Braque, it is claimed to date back to the Crusades. It
ｬs bred in the mountainous regions south of Toulouse, and by the
ｬd of the 18th century was popular throughout Europe.

ｬpearance Muscular, well-proportioned and clean-lined, it has a
ｬgish head, with plenty of black markings, and long, square
ｬzzle. Ears, medium length, pendant; eyes, dark to hazel; tail
ｬmmonly docked about two-thirds.

ｬight: 55-63cm (21-25in).

ｬight: 22-31kg (48-70lb).

ｬat: short, shiny.

ｬlour: white with black or dark gray patches and speckling.

ｬaracteristics A hardworking, active field dog, it can make an
ｬelligent, kindly companion, requiring plenty of exercise, minimum
ｬoming, and careful feeding to avoid overweight.

WEIMERANER

History This German silver ghost was known for many centuries and refined in the 19th century as the perfect hunting dog. It is fine-tuned to find, point, track and retrieve small and large game. There is a short- and a longhaired type.

Appearance A large-chested, well-muscled and proportioned dog it has a fairly long head, strong jaws and moderate stop. Ears, medium length, broad, slightly folded; eyes, blue-gray or amber; tail, half docked in the shorthair, tip docked in the long.

Height: 57-68cm (22-27in).

Weight: 32-38kg (70-85lb).

Coat: close and fine, or 2-5cm (1-2in) long with slight feathering.

Colour: silvery, metallic gray.

Characteristics Obedient, fearless, intelligent, it responds to firm training. Will make a good companion and pet if properly socialized and puppies selected from docile strains. Needs hard exercise, warmth when not working, light grooming.

ITALIAN POINTER/BRACCO ITALIANO

History Probably the oldest European gundog type, it is the progenitor of many setter and pointer breeds today.

Appearance Generally well built and vigorous, it has a long shapely head and pendant lips. Ears, medium length, pendant; eyes, yellow to chestnut; tail, commonly docked half to two-thirds.

Height: 55-67cm (22-26in).

Weight: 25-40kg (55-88lb).

Coat: short and fine.

Colour: white, white and orange, amber or chestnut markings and speckles.

Characteristics A rather undemonstrative dog, it is a hard worker in the field, docile and adaptable to most environments making a good family dog requiring minimum grooming, but plenty of exercise and careful training.

SPINONE/ITALIAN SPINONE/SPINONE ITALIANO/ITALIAN COARSEHAIRED POINTER

History A very ancient Italian gundog, its antecedents are lost in time but hound and pointer characteristics are now evident.

Appearance A muscular, solid dog it has a long, broad head with slight stop, strong jaws, very soft mouth. Ears, triangular, pendant, medium length; eyes, yellow to brown; tail, usually docked about half.

Height: 58-70cm (23-28in).
Weight: 28-37kg (62-82lb).
Coat: hard, thick, wiry, longer on face, oily.
Colour: orange or chestnut specks or markings on white, or white.

Characteristics Robust and good-natured, it is as adaptable to family life as it is to hunting. Good with children, it needs regular exercise and grooming.

HUNGARIAN VIZSLA/VISZLA

History Identified in the central plains of Hungary in the 18th century, it is of much older lineage and some claim the colour comes from the Turkish yellow dog. It was substantially redeveloped after the two World Wars, and there is also a wirehaired version.

Appearance A well muscled dog, it has a square muzzle and swish forehead. Ears, pendant, medium length; eyes, brown; tail, straight, often docked about one-third.

Height: 53-62cm (21-24in).
Weight: 22-28kg (49-52lb).
Coat: short and tight.
Colour: dark yellow, sometimes with chestnut sheen.

Characteristics An all-purpose hunting dog, it is remarkable for its elegant appearance, docility and trainability. Strong, adaptable and affectionate, it lives happily in family environment, requiring plenty of exercise and light grooming.

GERMAN WIREHAIRED POINTER/DRAHTAAR

History Bred in Germany this century from pointers, poodles, larger terriers and Airedale to produce a fine hunting dog on land or in the water. The Drahtaar Club maintains close controls on breeders.

Appearance Its muzzle is long and strong. Ears, medium length pendant; eyes, dark; tail, commonly docked about two-thirds.

Height: 56-67cm (22-26in).
Weight: 21-32kg (45-70lb).
Coat: rough textured.
Colour: dark to medium chestnut on white.
Characteristics Essentially a working dog, lively, obedient and patient, it is basically a one man dog and can be jealous particularly of other dogs. Requires plenty of exercise, regular grooming, sound trainin

WIREHAIRED POINTING GRIFFON/KORTHALS GRIFFON

History Developed by the Dutch breeder, E.K. Korthals, mainly from French Griffon Pointers, Otterhound, Setter, Pointer and Spaniels.

Appearance Has an attractive head with bushy eyebrows and moustache. Ears, pendant, medium length; eyes, yellow or blue; tail is often docked by about one-third.

Height: 50-60cm (20-24in).
Weight: 23kg (50lb).
Coat: thick, with long, wiry top coat, and soft, short under.
Colour: wide-ranging variations of steel gray and chestnut particolour.
Characteristics Essentially a

working dog with an exception sense of smell, it is patient and has a love of water. Good with children, affectionate, intelligent hardy and active, it requires ligh grooming and light trimming, and plenty of exercise.

50

CURLY-COATED RETRIEVER

History Probably the first breed to be used as a retriever particularly in water in England, is likely to have come from Irish water spaniels, poodles and setters.

Appearance A large, muscular dog, its head is long, wedge-shaped and clean. Ears, pendant; eyes, dark; tail, straight.
Height: 63-68cm (25-27in).
Weight: 32-36kg (70-80lb).
Coat: close, crisp curls.
Colour: black or liver.
Characteristics Bred to be hardy, for endurance and speed,

it has keen scent and sight, and a good mouth. Affectionate and loyal, it is a working dog that doubles as a good family dog and guard. It requires hard exercise, and the coat should be massaged damp rather than brushed or combed, and needs occasional trimming.

PUDELPOINTER/POODLE POINTER

History Developed at the end of the 19th century from shorthaired gundogs, pointers, and possibly the old, wooly Barbet, or Poodles. Better known today as the progenitor of the German Wirehaired Pointer, it is a fine sporting dog in its own right.

Appearance Strong muzzled, it has a deep forehead with whiskery eyebrows. Ears, pendant; eyes, yellow or

chestnut; tail, often docked.
Height: 60-65cm (24-26in).
Weight: 25-31kg (55-70lb).
Coat: thick, coarse, hard.
Colour: dark chestnut.
Characteristics A hardy, multi-purpose working dog, it is adaptable, docile and loyal. Lives well in family environment; requires hard exercise, moderate grooming.

STABYHOUN

History Originally bred in Friesland to control rats, by the end of the 18th century its qualities as a water dog and an efficient gundog were fully recognized in Holland.
Appearance Has a sturdy frame with longish back, the muzzle is strong and tapering. Ears, medium, hairy, pendant; eyes, light to dark brown; tail, long.
Height: up to 55cm (20in).

Weight: 15-20kg (33-44lb).
Coat: flat and sleek, with feathering.
Colour: black, blue, brown or orange with white.
Characteristics A popular working dog and pet in Holland it is easily trained, gentle and good natured with children. It requires plenty of exercise and moderate grooming.

LARGE MÜNSTERLÄNDER

History Developed in Germany from Spaniels and the German Longhaired Pointer as a dual purpose pointer and retriever at the turn of the century.
Appearance An alert, rather long head. Ears, pendant, fairly short and hairy; eyes, dark; tail straight and sometimes tip-docked.
Height: 58-63cm (23-25in).
Weight: 22-32kg (50-70lb).
Coat: sleek with some feathering.
Colour: blue roan, white with black markings and speckling.
Characteristics Primarily a working dog, it also makes a good guard dog, intelligent and hardy. Needs to be used and kept active.

The SMALL MÜNSTERLÄNDER is about 50cm (20in) and has similar ancestry but white and chestnut markings. It, too, is bred primarily as a dual purpose gundog.

AMERICAN WATER SPANIEL

History The Irish Water Spaniel and the Curly-coated Retriever are likely to have passed on the distinctive coat and colour.

Appearance A compact, well muscled frame, it has a wide head, pronounced stop and square muzzle. Ears, wide, long, pendant; eyes, hazel or chestnut; tail, medium length slightly curved.
Height: 38-45cm (15-18in).
Weight: 11-20kg (25-44lb).
Coat: thick, tight curls.

Colour: dark chocolate or liver.
Characteristics Loves water, fun loving and intelligent, it is a good worker, an effective guard, and good companion. Needs plenty of exercise and mental challenge, careful grooming with attention to ears.

IRISH WATER SPANIEL

History Water retrievers go back 1,000 years, or longer in Ireland, but this remarkable wildfowler only appeared in the mid 19th century.

Appearance The tallest of the spaniels, it is an agile powerful swimmer. Compact, almost barrel shaped in body, the head is domed, the face smooth, muzzle square. Ears, long, covered in curls; eyes, dark brown; tail, tapers, free of curls.
Height: 53-60cm (20-24in). **Weight:** 20-27kg (45-60lb).
Coat: crisp curls, dense undercoat, oily.
Colour: rich liver.
Characteristics A good-natured, intelligent, courageous working dog, it needs committed training to control independent nature in a domestic environment. Lives happily with the family, who must be prepared to put up with smelly coat when wet, and provide hard exercise and grooming.

53

GORDON SETTER

History Bred by the 4th Duke of Gordon in Scotland in the late 18th century.

Appearance Heavier frame than other setters and large, it has a rounded head and pronounced stop. Ears, long, pendant; eyes, brown; tail, may slightly curve.
Height: 55-64cm (22-25in).
Weight: 27-33kg (60-75lb).
Coat: long, silky, with feathering.

Colour: shiny black with tan markings.
Characteristics A determined working dog, intelligent and kindly, it makes a good, if large, family dog and guard. Strong willed, it requires consistent discipline, will overgrow strength if not fed properly when young, needs plenty of space for hard exercise and regular grooming.

ENGLISH SETTER

History Setter type dogs were used throughout Europe for five or more centuries before Edward Laverack established this breed in England in the mid 19th century.

Appearance An elegant, deceptively powerful dog, it has a long head and muzzle and pronounced stop. Show dogs vary from working strains. Ears, moderate length, hang in folds; eyes, dark hazel; tail, may curve.
Height: 60-68cm (24-27in).
Weight: 25-30kg (56-66lb).
Coat: long, silky, slightly wavy, with feathering.
Colour: white and black, lemon, orange or chestnut, or tricolour, and speckling.

Characteristics Active, lively, intelligent, it is a good-natured companion. Needs discipline to control exhuberance, plenty of exercise, regular grooming and occasional trimming. Tendency to become fat.

IRISH SETTER/IRISH RED SETTER

History The pure red setter was developed in Ireland from the red and White Setter in the 19th century; the breed suffered from over-specialization for the show ring, but efforts were then made to redeem this.

Appearance Built for speed, its balance, proportion and good musculature are key features; the head is long with pronounced stop and occiptal bump and long, squarish muzzle. Ears, long, pendant; eyes, hazel to dark brown; tail, straight and tapering.
Height: 62-68cm (25-27in).
Weight: 27-31kg (60-70lb).
Coat: flat, shiny, with feathering.
Colour: deep, rich chestnut, occasionally white streaks.
Characteristics Affectionate and friendly, this is a good family dog, but exuberant nature requires consistent discipline, plenty of exercise, and regular handling and grooming.

IRISH RED AND WHITE SETTER

History The original Irish setter, the Red and White was probably developed from the "setting" spaniels, British setters and bloodhound.

Appearance Slightly smaller and lighter than the Irish Setter, proportionally it has a heavier body and broader head and it is red and white in colour.

Characteristics This good-natured field dog makes a charming family dog, requiring plenty of exercise, consistent early training to control bounciness, and moderate grooming.

55

GOLDEN RETRIEVER
History All Golden Retrievers originate from a litter bred by Lord Tweedmouth in Scotland from a yellow wavy-coated retriever and Tweed Water Spaniel in the mid 19th century.
Appearance A deep-chested, strong, well-balanced dog, it has a broad head and strong muzzle and dark nose. Ears, medium length pendant; eyes, dark; tail, straight, feathered.
Height: 51-61cm (21-24in).
Weight: 27-34kg (60-75lb).
Coat: wavy and glossy with generous feathering.
Colour: cream to golden.
Characteristics A hardy, obedient working dog, it is also exceptionally gentle making a very popular and successful family pet. It needs plenty of exercise, prefers a cool environment, and regular grooming with attention to feet.

FLAT-COATED RETRIEVER
History Labrador, setter, pointer, Newfoundland and spaniel blood gave rise to the old, British Wavy-coated Retriever which in the late 19th century was crossed with the Collie for the distinctive coat.
Appearance Strong overall musculature, and a fairly broad head with gradual taper to strong muzzle. Ears, quite small, pendant; eyes dark; tail, straight.
Height: 56-58cm (22-23in).
Weight: 27-32kg (60-70lb).
Coat: straight, dense, sometimes wavy, feathering.
Colour: black or liver.
Characteristics Very hardy and adaptable, this is a good working dog and family pet with an intelligent, affectionate nature. It needs plenty of exercise to keep figure, and moderate grooming with attention to feet in bad weather.

56

CHESAPEAKE BAY RETRIEVER

History Developed from local duck shooting dogs and possibly from Newfoundland dogs rescued from a shipwreck off Maryland, US, in 1807, these "Chesapeake Bay Ducking Dogs" became standardized towards the end of the 19th century.
Appearance Typically broad and strong. Ears, pendant; eyes, pale brown; tail, a thick rudder.
Height: 53-68cm (21-26in).
Weight: 25-34kg (55-75lb).

Coat: tight, wavy outer coat, woolly under coat, oily to repel water.
Colour: dried hay to dark chestnut, sometimes white on chest.
Characteristics Unquestionably a working dog, it is very hardy, courageous, cheerful, obedient, occasionally pugnacious, and loves water. Prefers a cool environment, moderate grooming, plenty of exercise.

LABRADOR RETRIEVER

History Originally bred by Newfoundland fisherman to retrieve from the sea, it was brought to England in the early 19th century and established as a retriever from land or water.
Appearance This popular dog has a strong, deep body with sturdy limbs, powerful jaws, broad head and noticeable stop. Ears, medium length, pendant; eyes, brown or hazel; tail, densely furred ("otter tail") strong and sturdy.
Height: 54-57cm (21½-22½ in).
Weight: 24-36kg (55-75lb).
Coat: straight, short, hard top, and dense waterproof under.
Colour: black, yellow to golden, liver.
Characteristics An excellent retriever, its intelligent, gentle, biddable nature makes it a fine family pet being very fond of children. Naturally exuberant, it needs firm early training, and must have plenty of exercise to avoid getting fat, and regular grooming.

57

COCKER SPANIEL, ENGLISH
History Spaniels have been identifiable in Europe since the 14th century. In Britain the Cocker emerged in the 19th century as a dog to flush and retrieve game.
Appearance A strong, compact body sloping slightly to the tail, it has a handsome head with distinct stop and square muzzle. Ears, long, hairy, hang from eye level; eyes, soft, dark brown; tail, commonly docked.
Height: 38-41cm (15-16in).

Weight: 10-12.7kg (22-28lb).
Coat: flat, silky, wavy.
Colour: many variables including black, roan, golden, tricolour or particolour.
Characteristics An active field dog, it makes a cheerful and popular companion and family pet requiring plenty of exercise as easily gets fat, regular grooming with attention to ears, and feet, and occasional trimming. Parents of puppies from solid colour strains should be checked for temperament.

COCKER SPANIEL, AMERICAN
History Derived from the English Cocker, and selectively bred for hunting conditions in America requiring a smaller dog.
Appearance A compact, sturdy frame, back sloping to tail, it has a well rounded head with pronounced brow, and broad rather short muzzle. Ears, long, set at eye level; eyes, dark hazel to black; tail, commonly docked.
Height: 34-39cm (14-15in).
Weight: 10-12.7kg (22-28lb).
Coat: long, flat, silky, slightly wavy, with feathering.
Colour: many variables from lightest buff to black, tricolour and particolours.
Characteristics Sporty and affectionate, it can be trained easily and is a good family dog requiring plenty of exercise, grooming and trimming, with attention to ears and feet.

58

BRITTANY SPANIEL/BRITTANY EPAGNEUL BRETON/BRETON SPANIEL

History Somewhere between a setter and a spaniel, it developed in northern France and emerged as a distinct breed in Brittany in the 19th century for pointing, flushing and retrieving.

Appearance Generally square, muscular body, it has a wedge-shaped head, stop, and fairly short muzzle. Ears, quite short, pendant; eyes, amber to brown; tail, naturally short or docked.

Height: 45-50cm (17-20in).
Weight: 15-18kg (35-44lb).
Coat: fairly thick, silky, slightly wavy, with feathering.
Colour: orange or red (occasionally black) on white.
Characteristics A fearless, hardy, intelligent dog, it adapts well to family life and is a popular pet. It needs good, long walks, moderate grooming, firm but gentle training.

CLUMBER SPANIEL

History Despite its English name, the Clumber was bred in France by the Duc de Noailles to eat and retrieve. The entire kennel was shipped to Clumber Park at the start of the French Revolution and stayed there.

Appearance Square, heavy dogs they have rather short, sturdy legs and large feet. The head is very broad with distinct stop and heavy muzzle with well-developed lips. Ears, broad, medium length, pendant; eyes, deep sunk, dark amber; tail, short, well feathered.

Height: 41-46cm (16-18in).
Weight: 25-31kg (55-70lb).
Coat: thick, straight and silky with feathering.
Colour: creamy white with lemon or orange markings, slightly speckled muzzle.
Characteristics Strong, willing, built for endurance rather than speed, has an exceptional nose, makes a good pet being silent and good humoured with children. Requires plenty of exercise, regular grooming.

ENGLISH SPRINGER SPANIEL

History Springers were bred to "spring" game for falconers and are probably the oldest spaniels.

Appearance Compact, though fairly long-legged and generally stronger than other spaniels, the broad head has a marked stop, strong jaws and well-defined lips. Ears, long, pendant; eyes, dark hazel; tail, usually docked.

Height: 50cm (20in).

Weight: 22-24kg (49-53lb).

Coat: close, weather resistant, quite soft with feathering.

Colour: liver or black and white.

Characteristics A willing and affectionate worker, it is popular as a pet, but requires patient and firm handling to control exuberance, rigorous exercise, regular grooming with attention to ears.

THE WELSH SPRINGER SPANIEL is very similar, but a bit smaller and lighter, and always red and white in colour.

SUSSEX SPANIEL

History An acknowledged breed distinct to Sussex in England by the mid 19th century meeting a demand for stamina rather than speed in dense country.

Appearance The long look of this dog is deceptive, it has a rolling gait, is solid, compact and muscular with broad head, pronounced stop, heavy brows and wide deep muzzle. Ears, medium length, quite large; eyes, hazel; tail, usually docked.

Height: 33-38cm (13-15in).

Weight: 18-23kg (40-50lb).

Coat: flat, abundant, weather-resistant undercoat, feathering.

Colour: liver with golden glint

Characteristics A hardy, patient, active and, unusually, vocal, gundog, it makes a fine companion and family dog, but needs plenty of exercise and regular grooming with care for feet and ears.

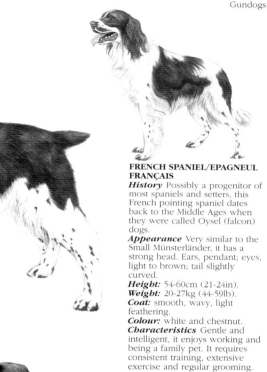

FRENCH SPANIEL/EPAGNEUL FRANÇAIS

History Possibly a progenitor of most spaniels and setters, this French pointing spaniel dates back to the Middle Ages when they were called Oysel (falcon) dogs.

Appearance Very similar to the Small Münsterländer, it has a strong head. Ears, pendant; eyes, light to brown; tail slightly curved.

Height: 54-60cm (21-24in).

Weight: 20-27kg (44-59lb).

Coat: smooth, wavy, light feathering.

Colour: white and chestnut.

Characteristics Gentle and intelligent, it enjoys working and being a family pet. It requires consistent training, extensive exercise and regular grooming.

LD SPANIEL

tory Separated as a breed n the Cocker Spaniel in the 19th century, it is heavier l longer in body proportionate he legs, and is adapted to iting over open country.

earance The body is well-anced, its head is slightly ned with distinct occiput, and g, firm muzzle. Ears, quite g, hairy; eyes, dark hazel or stnut; tail, straight, usually docked.

Height: about 46cm (18in).

Weight: 16-22kg (35-49lb).

Coat: flat to wavy, thick, silky.

Colour: black, liver, mahogany red, or roan, sometimes tan markings.

Characteristics Easy and reliable in the field, it makes an affectionate family pet, but not adaptable to city life; requires plentiful exercise, and regular grooming with attention to ears.

61

Hounds

BORZOI/RUSSIAN WOLFHOUND

History Middle Eastern in origin, bred in Russia by crossing with hardier breeds, and used by Russian royal families to chase and kill wolves.

Appearance A graceful, powerful gazehound it has a slightly arched back, long head and strong jaws. Ears, small, semi-erect when alert; eyes, dark; tail, long, carried low.

Height: 68-75cm (26-30in).
Weight: 34-48kg (75-105lb).
Coat: long, wavy, with feathering.
Colour: most colour combinations, often with white predominating.

Characteristics Generally calm, rather sensitive and aloof, and loyal, it makes a good, if large, family dog when consistently controlled, extensively exercised and well fed. Requires moderate grooming.

SALUKI/GAZELLE HOUND/PERSIAN GREYHOUND

History Valued by the Bedouin for hunting and hawking, it is one of the earliest breeds.

Appearance Gracefully built for speed and strength, its back is fairly broad and arched, and the elegant neck supports a long head with broad forehead. Ears, long, mobile; eyes, hazel to dark brown; tail, gently curved.

Height: 58-71cm (23-28in).
Weight: 13-30kg (29-66lb).
Coat: soft, silky with feathering; no feathering on smoothhaired variety.
Colour: white, cream, fawn, golden, red, or gray/grizzle.

Characteristics Friendly and loyal, its rather sensitive nature demands gentle, consistent training and handling. Likes to stretch itself in open country, it must have plentiful exercise and regular grooming.

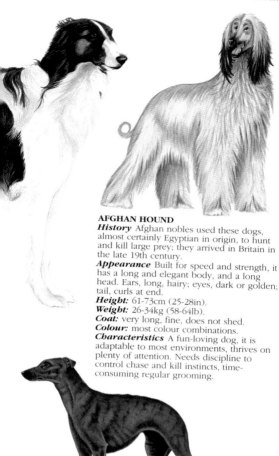

AFGHAN HOUND
History Afghan nobles used these dogs, almost certainly Egyptian in origin, to hunt and kill large prey; they arrived in Britain in the late 19th century.
Appearance Built for speed and strength, it has a long and elegant body, and a long head. Ears, long, hairy; eyes, dark or golden; tail, curls at end.
Height: 61-73cm (25-28in).
Weight: 26-34kg (58-64lb).
Coat: very long, fine, does not shed.
Colour: most colour combinations.
Characteristics A fun-loving dog, it is adaptable to most environments, thrives on plenty of attention. Needs discipline to control chase and kill instincts, time-consuming regular grooming.

REYHOUND
istory This very old Middle Eastern sighthound is probably closest the earliest form of gazehound built for racing and hunting.
ppearance Muscular, deep-chested, long, lean and well-balanced, has a long head and powerful jaws. Ears, small, semi-erect; eyes, rk; tail, carried low, slightly curved.
eight: 69-76cm (27-31in).
eight: 27-32kg (60-70lb).
at: short, tight and silky.
lour: black, white, red, blue, brindle, and particolours.
aracteristics Hardy and affectionate, it is primarily a coursing, cing dog that needs firm control when kept as a pet in the home here it is neat, loyal and affectionate, requiring only moderate ercise – if not worked – and minimum grooming.

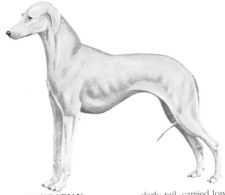

SLOUGHI/ARABIAN GREYHOUND

History Like the Greyhound, its ancestry lies in ancient Egypt and it is a popular racing dog in France and North Africa.
Appearance Tall, lean and built for speed, its head is moderately long with flatish forehead and slightly pointed muzzle. Ears, medium length, drooping; eyes,
dark; tail, carried low.
Height: 55-75cm (22-30in).
Weight: 30-32kg (66-70lb).
Coat: fine, smooth.
Colour: sand, fawn, off-white, black and tan, or brindle.
Characteristics Docile and obedient, it is a good family dog needing plentiful exercise, minimum grooming, and warmth.

IBIZAN HOUND

History The likeness of this dog is seen on the tombs of Egyptian Pharaohs and it has altered little since isolated on Ibiza where it was taken by the Carthaginians in the 6th century BC.
Appearance Compact, muscular, it has a long narrow head. Ears, large, erect; eyes, light amber; tail, long, thin, slightly curved.
Height: 57-66cm (22-26in).
Weight: 19-22kg (42-50lb).
Coat: rough or smooth; thin-skinned.
Colour: solid white, tan, or red, or with white markings.
Characteristics A natural hunter, it is agile, spirited and good-natured, responding well to gentle training to make a good companion and house dog requiring moderate exercise and minimum grooming.

The PHARAOH HOUND has a similar history and many of the characteristics of the Ibizan, but is exclusively smoothhaired and tan in colour, with occasional white patches, and amber eyes.

WHIPPET

History Recognized as a breed at the end of the 19th century, its origins in the north of England are rather obscure though it undoubtedly owes its lines and grace to Middle Eastern sighthounds. It was used for racing and hunting by working folk, its size making it easy to keep. The coarsehaired variety is very rarely seen.

Appearance Deep-chested, elegant, muscular, it has a slightly arched back, long, lean head and fine muzzle. Ears, small rose-shaped; eyes, brown; tail, thin, carried low.

Height: 43-46cm (17^1/$_2$-18^1/$_2$ in).
Weight: 5-12kg (12-28lb).
Coat: fine, short.
Colour: any shades and mixtures.

Characteristics Very fast, gentle, friendly, obedient and neat, it is a popular pet. Loves to stretch its legs, but needs only moderate exercise and minimum grooming, but should be kept dry and warm.

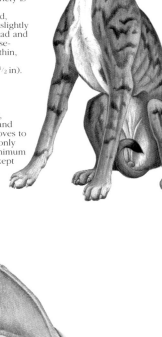

RHODESIAN RIDGEBACK/AFRICAN LION HOUND

History Developed with other crosses by Boer farmers from an ancient Hottentot ridged dog to hunt lion in southern Africa.

Appearance The wrong-facing ridge of hair tapering down the spine from the shoulder is the distinctive feature of this large, well-proportioned hunting dog with its broad head and strong jaws. Ears, rather wide, pendant; eyes, tone with coat; tail, strong with slight curve.

Height: 61-68.5cm (24-27in).
Weight: 29-34kg (65-75lb).
Coat: thick, short, glossy.
Colour: wheaten to red.
Characteristics A determined, courageous hunter, when well trained it makes a good guard and family dog being obedient and gentle with children. It needs regular exercise, but minimum grooming.

IRISH WOLFHOUND

History Existing in Ireland before Roman times, this large, strong dog was used to hunt and kill wolves. Virtually disappearing by the early 19th century, it was redeveloped using Great Dane, Deerhound and Borzoi in the mid 19th century.

Appearance Heavier, though similar in appearance to the Deerhound, its head is long and strong. Ears, quite small, folded back, semi-erect when alert; eyes, dark; tail, slightly curved.

Height: 71-79cm (28-31in).

Weight: 40-54kg (88-119lb).

Coat: wiry, rough, shaggy, with moustache and beard.

Colour: dark to light gray, brindle, fawn, sandy red, or yellow.

Characteristics Reliable, intelligent, friendly, this is a good guard and family dog being gentle with children. It needs firm early training on leash and to prevent animal chasing, plenty of space in and out of the home, plentiful exercise, gentle, but regular grooming.

DEERHOUND/SCOTTISH DEERHOUND

History A very old breed, developed in the Scottish highlands to stalk and hunt deer.

Appearance Larger, but similar to Greyhound in form, the coat is a distinguishing feature. Ears, short, folded back, semi-erect when alert; eyes, dark; tail, long, curving in movement.

Height: 71-76cm (28-30in).

Weight: 30-48kg (65-105lb).

Coat: shaggy, medium length, moustache and beard.

Colour: fawn to dark gray, or brindle.

Characteristics Loyal, gentle, affectionate, it makes a good, if large, family dog requiring moderate exercise and grooming and quite modest meals for a dog of its size.

OTTERHOUND

History Probably French in origin, and known in Britain since the 14th century, it combines traits of hound and terrier in pursuit through marsh and water of otter.

Appearance A large dog, it has plenty of muscle and strength, the head is large, fairly narrow with strong jaws. Ears, long, pendant; eyes, dark; tail, slightly curving.

Height: 56-67cm (22-27in).

Weight: 30-53kg (66-115lb).

Coat: rough outer, water-resistant, woolly inner.

Colour: most hound colours, but lighter shades more common.

Characteristics A true hound in character, it is amiable, intelligent and brave with keen sense of smell. Needs firm handling, but will make a good country companion where space, plentiful exercise and careful grooming are supplied.

BLOODHOUND/ST HUBERT HOUND

History The breed originated with St Hubert at his abbey in Belgium from scent hounds going back some 2,000 years. He aimed to produce a dog that would scent and track quarry over considerable distance and not harm it.

Appearance A massive dog with pronounced folds of its loose skin over head and neck; the head is large and long, lips droopy. Ears, very long; eyes, deep sunk, yellow or hazel; tail, long, gently curved.

Height: 58-69cm (24-27in).

Weight: 40-48kg (88-105lb).

Coat: short, dense, silky.

Colour: black and tan, liver and tan, or red, occasionally white markings.

Characteristics The powers of scent of this gentle giant are proverbial, and it can make a good-natured family dog. Completely unsuitable for an urban environment requiring considerable and regular exercise to keep fit; it is happiest and almost unstoppable when on scent. Minimum grooming, but special attention to skin folds.

American COONHOUNDS – Black and Tan, Bluetick, English and Redbone – were bred from European hounds to hunt racoon.

67

BEAGLE
History These small pack hounds for hare hunting date back to the 16th century, possibly using spaniel blood to decrease the size of Foxhounds and Harriers.
Appearance Short, strong, and compact in body it has a nicely proportioned, broad head, pronounced stop and squarish muzzle. Ears, medium length, pendant; eyes, hazel to brown; tail (stern), straight, carried high.
Height: 33-40cm (13-16in).
Weight: 8.2-13.6kg (18-30lb).
Coat: thick, smooth.
Colour: variable tri- or bicolour, white tail tip.
Characteristics Active, cheerful and friendly, it is a good family dog, but requires firm training and handling to control wilfulness when on scent, plenty of exercise, minimum grooming.

BASSET HOUND (RIGHT)
History French in origin, developed from mutant hounds producing dwarf pups and some Bloodhound crossing to hunt in dense undergrowth.
Appearance Body is long, broad and deep with short, strong legs; head has slightly furrowed brows, prominent occiput, pendulous top lip. Ears very long; eyes, hazel or brown; tail, long with slight curve.
Height: 33-38cm (13-15in).
Weight: 18-23kg (40-51lb).
Coat: smooth, short, close.
Colour: variable bi- and tricolours.
Characteristics Lively, affectionate, good with children it requires plenty of steady exercise (monitored during growing stage to avoid spine strain), minimum grooming. Can be stubborn when on scent.

PETIT BASSET GRIFFON VENDÉEN/SMALL GRIFFON VENDÉEN

History There are four varieties of Griffon Vendéen: The Grand; the Briquet; the Grand Basset; and the Petit Basset. All originated as hunting dogs in the Vendée region of France. The first three are essentially still working hunting dogs, but the fourth has gained in popularity as a pet and was officially recognized in 1950.

Appearance Has a compact frame, longish back, short legs, long muzzle and shaggy brows and muzzle. Ears, medium length; eyes, brown; tail, long, slightly curved.

Height: 33-38cm (13-15in).
Weight: 11-16kg (25-35lb).
Coat: short, coarse, thick.
Colour: variable tri- and bicolour on predominant white.

Characteristics Its devil-may-care, lively nature has won it favour as a family dog being friendly with children and intelligent. It requires plentiful exercise and minimum grooming; can be wilful when on scent.

BASSET FAUVE DE BRETAGNE/ TAWNY BRITTANY BASSETT

History Developed in France from Basset Vendéen and Griffon Fauve de Bretagne for field and close cover work, it is now gaining favour as a pet.

Appearance Short-legged, it has a long but compact, muscular body, and longish head. Ears, medium length; eyes, brown; tail, long, slight curve.

Height: 32-36cm (13-14in).
Weight: 16-18kg (36-40lb).
Coat: short, coarse, thick.
Colour: fawn to gold, or red.

Characteristics Lively, affectionate and gentle with children, it needs minimum grooming, plentiful exercise though can be stubborn when on scent.

DACHSHUNDS

History German in origin, these small, short-legged dogs were bred to hunt foxes, badgers and rabbits. There are three types: smoothhaired, longhaired, and wirehaired; as well as miniature versions of all three.

Appearance Deep-chested, short-legged, long-bodied, the head is finely modelled with a strong jaw. Ears, quite long, pendant; eyes, dark; tail, long and tapering.

Height: 12-22cm (5-9in).

Weight: 9kg (20lb); Miniature 4kg (9lb).

Coat: short, silky and smooth; o soft, straight or slightly wavy; or short and wiry.

Colour: all colours, solid and bicolour most common.

Characteristics Active, lively, affectionate pets, they are stubborn hunters if not controlled and can be noisy. They require only moderate exercise, but careful feeding to avoid overweight and strain on spine.

BASENJI/CONGO DOG (RIGHT)

History These small hunting dogs were "discovered" in Central Africa by explorers in the 1870s, and undoubtedly go back to the earliest Pariah dogs.

Appearance Firm, light, and upright in body, it has a flat, wrinkled chiselled head. Ears, medium, erect; eyes, dark; tail, curled right over.

Height: 40-42.5cm (16-17in).

Weight: 10-11kg (22-24lb).

Coat: short and silky.

Colour: red, or black, or black and tan, with white markings.

Characteristics Cheerful, intelligent, good with children, it is adaptable to most environments, and barkless (it has a sort of yodel). It is inclined to scrap with other dogs if not given firm discipline. Requires regular exercise, minimum grooming.

WEDISH DACHSBRACKE/ DREVER

History German in origin,
probably combining Dachshund
and other pack hounds in its
ancestry, it has been developed
in Sweden as a popular hunter of
hare and fox.

Appearance A muscular, long-
bodied little dog. Ears, medium
length, pendant; eyes, chestnut;
tail, long, straight.

Height: 31-37cm (12-15in).

Weight: 15kg (33lb).

Coat: short, thick.

Colour: all colours usually with
markings.

Characteristics Essentially a
hunting dog, it is obedient and
kindly with children, requiring
regular exercise, minimum
grooming.

The WESTPHALIAN
DACHSBRACKE was developed
in Germany from short-legged
pack hounds and possibly
dachshunds for keen scent and
hunting prowess, but is gaining
popularity as a family dog
because of its neat habit and
generous nature.

Working (Herding) Dogs

GERMAN SHEPHERD DOG/ ALSATIAN

History At the end of the 19th century this breed was developed i
Germany as the ideal shepherd dog. Its popularity increased hugel
as its qualities in other fields such as police, military, hunting, and
guarding became apparent.

Appearance Very supple, deep-chested, and muscular, it has a
broad head tapering to strong jaws. Ears, erect, pointed; eyes, dark
tail, carried low with slight curve.

Height: 55-65cm (22-24in).

Weight: 35-40kg (77-85lb).

Coat: weather resistant, flat outer, thick inner, ruff; length varies.

Colour: mixtures of gray, yellow, and black.

Characteristics Very intelligent and quick to learn, this is a reliabl
house and family dog though can be over-protective if not well
socialized. It requires consistent training, plentiful exercise and
regular grooming. Some inbred strains can show undue nervousnes
and unreliability.

GROENENDAEL/BELGIAN SHEEPDOG

History Developed in Belgium
in the late 19th century.

Appearance Has a strong, deep-
chested body with a lean head.
Ears, triangular, erect; eyes,
brown; tail, long, straight.

Height: 58-63cm (23-25in).

Weight: 28kg (62lb).

Coat: long, sleek, feathering.

Colour: shiny black.

Characteristics Essentially a
working dog used by farmers
and police, it is generally docile,
intelligent, and gentle with
children, though, some can be
over timid. Requires firm, but
gentle training, plenty of working
exercise, minimum grooming.

MALINOIS/BELGIAN SHEEPDOG

History Shares ancestry with the other Belgian sheepdogs, acquiring separate breed status in 1891.
Appearance Deep-chested, strong, and athletic, it has a fairly long, lean head with slight stop. Ears, triangular, erect; eyes, brown; tail, long.
Height: 60cm (24in).
Weight: 24-27kg (55-60lb).
Coat: short, dense.
Colour: black-tinged fawn, dark on muzzle.
Characteristics Hardy, adaptable to both farm and guard work, it is an intelligent dog, but is naturally protective requiring firm training and control. Unsuited to an urban environment, it requires

minimum grooming.

The LAEKENOIS has a distinctively different coat to the other Belgian sheepdogs being rough, harsh and shaggy.

TERVUERIN/BELGIAN SHEEPDOG

History Sharing the same background as the other Belgian sheepdogs, it was given separate breed status by Professor Reul of the Belgian faculty of Veterinary sciences in 1891.
Appearance Robust and elegant, its head is well-proportioned and long with slight stop. Ears, triangular, erect; eyes, brown; tail, long, plumed.
Height: 58-63cm (23-25in).

Weight: 28kg (62lb).
Coat: thick, long, sleek, with feathering and ruff.
Colour: warm fawn with black shading, black mask.
Characteristics Intelligent, and strongly protective, it makes a good guard but is best suited to a working rather than domestic environment. It requires plentiful exercise, moderate grooming.

SMOOTH COLLIE/SCOTCH COLLIE

History Has the same background as the Rough Collie.
Appearance Resembles the Rough in everything except coat.
Height: 51-66cm (20-26in).
Weight: 23-34kg (50-75lb).
Coat: short, flat outer, dense undercoat.
Colour: sable and white, tricolour, blue merle.
Characteristics Bright, mild-natured and neat, it makes a good companion and family dog, requiring only minimum grooming, but plenty of exercise.

ROUGH COLLIE

History Recognized as a breed in Scotland in the 19th century, its origins are obscure, though the type dates back several hundred years.
Appearance Deep-chested, strong, long bodied, it has a well-proportioned head tapering to long, round muzzle. Ears, small, semi-erect when alert; eyes, dark (merle may have blue or both); tail, has slight upward tilt.
Height: 51-66cm (20-26in).
Weight: 23-34kg (50-75lb).
Coat: long, dense, harsh outer and soft, furry under, substantial mane, feathering.
Colour: sable and white, tricolour, blue merle.
Characteristics Active, intelligent, obedient, it is a good family dog, though occasionally over-protective. Requires plenty of exercise, and considerable grooming.

SHETLAND SHEEPDOG

History Only recognized as a breed in 1907, it is thought it owes its origins to a King Charles Spaniel, and Spitz and Icelandic dogs carried on fishing boats.
Appearance It has a graceful, well-proportioned, sturdy body and a fine wedge-shaped head. Ears, semi-erect when alert; eyes, dark brown (blue permissible in merles); tail, has upward sweep.
Height: 33-41cm (13-16in).

Weight: 6-7kg (14-16lb).
Coat: long, straight, harsh outer, with soft under, long mane, feathering.
Colour: many variations of tricolour, fawn to red, black, blue merles, with white.
Characteristics Affectionate and intelligent, it makes a successful family dog, but can be over-protective if not socialized. It requires regular grooming, and moderate exercise.

BORDER COLLIE

History Developed in the Scottish Highlands for herding over hard terrain, this dog is judged in the field on its success as a worker, though some dogs are bred for the show ring.
Appearance Deep-chested, strong and agile, it has a rather broad head, perceptible stop, long, square muzzle. Ears, small, erect or semi-erect; eyes, usually dark; tail, slightly curved.
Height: 48-56cm (19-22in).

Weight: 16-23kg (35-50lb).
Coat: weatherproof, dense and coarse, or dense and sleek.
Colour: many variations of black, tan and white.
Characteristics Bred to work, extremely intelligent and trainable, though some can be over-excitable, and herding instinct will include human family and other pets. It requires regular grooming and active, regular exercise.

KELPIE AUSTRALIAN KELPIE/BARB

History Bred by early farmers in
Australia to work in extreme
conditions, these dogs show the
influence of the 18th century
black, and black and tan sheep
dogs of the north of England.
Appearance Compact, strong
and agile, its head is fox-like
with strong jaws. Ears, erect,
pointed; eyes, brown; tail, has
slight curve.
Height: 43-50cm (17-20in).
Weight: 9-14kg (20-30lb).
Coat: short, smooth.
Colour: black and tan, red,
black, or blue.
Characteristics Bred and used
as a working dog, it is friendly
and obedient. Unsuited to
restricted environments, it needs
plenty of exercise, minimum
grooming.

The AUSTRALIAN SHEPHERD
is in fact an American breed
incorporating Pyrenean Shepherd
and is an intelligent worker.

ANATOLIAN SHEPHERD DOG/KARABASH

History Descended from
Mastiffs of the Middle East, this
old breed was used in Turkey
both to protect herds and for
combat.
Appearance Particularly
powerful in the front, this large
dog has a big, broad head, and
squarish, strong jaws. Ears, short,
pendant; eyes, light brown; tail,
long, curved.
Height: 66-76cm (26-30in).
Weight: 41-68kg (90-150lb).

Coat: short, dense.
Colour: cream to fawn, or
brindle; sometimes darker face
and ears.
Characteristics Tough,
intelligent and very protective,
though gentle with its family, the
dog requires firm, consistent
socialization and handling,
plentiful exercise, minimum
grooming. Too powerful, to be
kept as a pet.

AUSTRALIAN CATTLE DOG/ AUSTRALIAN QUEENSLAND HEELER/BLUE HEELER

History Developed in Australia in the mid 19th century for hard, fast cattle herding, it includes amongst its ancestors the Dingo and Collie.
Appearance Has a compact, long frame, rather pointed head and strong jaws. Ears, erect, pointed; eyes, brown; tail, straight.
Height: 43-46cm (16-19in).
Weight: 16-23kg (35-50lb).

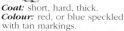

Coat: short, hard, thick.
Colour: red, or blue speckled with tan markings.
Characteristics This intelligent, agile, hardy, working and guard dog is not suited to a wholly domestic existence requiring extensive exercise and consistent training and handling, though little grooming. Has a habit of nipping at heels, hence its often used local name of heeler.

ESTRELA MOUNTAIN DOG/ PORTUGUESE SHEEPDOG

History Used in the mountainous Estrela region of Portugal for many centuries: guarding, hunting, herding and hauling.
Appearance A large, muscular dog, it has a broad, long head and strong jaws. Ears, small, folded; eyes, dark; tail, thick.
Height: 58-72cm (23-28in).
Weight: 40-50kg (88-110lb).
Coat: short or long, coarse, thick outer, dense undercoat. Dense feathering on long coats.
Colour: fawn, gray, tan and black, brindle, or mixture.
Characteristics Very powerful, intelligent and hardy, it requires firm discipline and socialization from an early age. A loyal companion, it is essentially a farm dog requiring plenty of exercise and moderate grooming.

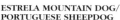

MAREMMA SHEEPDOG
History Known and used in Italy for as long as 2,000 years, it probably originated with the white Hungarian sheepdogs.
Appearance Agile, strong and large, it has a stately head. Ears, small, triangular, pendant; eyes, brown; tail, long.
Height: 60-73cm (24-29in).
Weight: 30-45kg (66-99lb).
Coat: long, thick, slightly wavy, denser on neck, thick undercoat feathering.
Colour: white.
Characteristics Primarily a working dog of intelligent but independent spirit. Affectionate and protective of its flock and it human family, it is essentially a country dog requiring hard work and exercise, and only moderate grooming.

PYRENEAN MOUNTAIN DOG/GREAT PYRENEES
History Developed in France over many centuries to protect mountain sheep from wolves, as general guards, and for mountain rescue work. It is descended from Tibetan Mastiffs which go back to at least 1,000 years BC.
Appearance Well-proportioned, large and strong, it has a broad head with medium length muzzle. Ears, triangular, pendant; eyes, amber brown; tail, slightly curving. Has double dew-claws.
Height: 64-81cm (25-32in).
Weight: 41-57kg (90-125lb).
Coat: long, thick, wavy or straight outer coat, fine and thick under, mane.
Colour: white, or with pale markings.
Characteristics Loyal, affectionate and hard-working, it is an adaptable though occasionally over-protective family dog. It require firm early training, plenty of space, food, stimulating exercise, moderate grooming.

SAINT BERNARD

History The Hospice of St Bernard, high in the Swiss Alps, gave its name to the breed and gave rise to the legend of its finding and reviving, with kegs of brandy, travellers lost in the snow. The Tibetan Mastiff is clearly represented in its ancestry.

Appearance Large and powerful, it has a massive head. Ears, medium length, pendant; eyes, deep, dark, with drooping lower lids; tail, slightly curved.

Height: 65-91cm (25-36in).

Weight: 50-55kg (110-121lb).

Coat: medium length, thick, flat with feathering, or, in shorthaired, short and dense.

Colour: orange, mahogany, or red-brindle, with white patches.

Characteristics Intelligent, dignified, patient with children, it makes a good family dog where space and large meals are available. Requires reasonable exercise and careful grooming.

KUVASZ

History Middle Eastern in origin, it was developed over centuries in Hungary.

Appearance Large, sturdy and well-balanced, it has a well-proportioned head with distinct stop. Ears, medium, folded; eyes, dark; tail, has slight curve.

Height: 66-75cm (26-30in).

Weight: 50kg (110lb).

Coat: quite long, short on head and feet, straight or wavy with fine undercoat.

Colour: white or ivory.

Characteristics Affection for children and kindly nature, complement its agility, strength and intelligence. Requires firm training and socialization, plenty of exercise, moderate grooming.

BOUVIER DES FLANDRES/BELGIAN CATTLE DOG

History Used as a cattle drover in Flanders in the 19th century, the breed was recognized in 1912. It almost disappeared in the First World War, but was re-established in Antwerpes.

Appearance A compact, powerful, upright dog it has a broad head and strong jaws. Ears, pointed; eyes, dark; tail, commonly docked.

Height: 66-70cm (23-27in).
Weight: 40kg (88lb).
Coat: harsh, rough outer, fine soft inner, weather resistant, beard and moustache.

Colour: from fawn to black, gray, or brindle, sometimes white star on chest.

Characteristics Hardy, courageous, obedient and good-natured, though bred to work it adapts well to family life, but requires careful training and socialization to avoid over-protectiveness. Needs plenty of energetic exercise, careful grooming, occasional trimming.

BRIARD/BERGER DE BRIE

History Like all the European herding dogs, it has a long history. It evolved in the Brie region of France, and was recognized as a breed in the early 19th century.

Appearance Well-proportioned, rugged and strong with a longish head, it has squarish powerful jaws. Ears, short, semi-erect, in some countries docked; eyes, dark; tail, slightly curved, or docked.

Height: 56-68cm (22-27in).
Weight: 35kg (75lb).
Coat: weather resistant, long, coarse.

Colour: black, gray or fawn, occasionally tipped with black, moustache, beard and brows.

Characteristics Hardy, lively, intelligent, affectionate, it is a

good worker and family dog when well trained. Some strains show over-sensitivity and require careful socialization. Plentiful exercise is essential, but only moderate grooming.

80

BERNESE MOUNTAIN DOG

History Of ancient lineage, it was recorded as a draught dog in Berne over 200 years, ago.

Appearance Deep-chested, large, strong and compact, it has a strong, straight muzzle. Ears, medium length, triangular, pendant; eyes, dark; tail, has slight curve.

Height: 58-70cm (23-28in).

Weight: 40kg (88lb).

Coat: long, soft, silky, slightly wavy, with feathering.

Colour: tricolour – mainly black with specific white and rich tan markings.

Characteristics Good-natured, gentle, affectionate, it copes happily with hard work and children. It needs firm early training, plenty of space and exercise and regular grooming. Prefers cooler conditions.

PICARDY SHEEPDOG/BERGER PICARD

History Possibly going back to Celtic times, it is similar to many sheepdogs in Germany and Holland and works equally with cattle and sheep.

Appearance Sturdy and rugged, it has a large head and strong muzzle. Ears, erect; eyes, dark; tail, slightly curved.

Height: 53-63cm (21-25in).

Weight: 27-32kg (60-70lb).

Coat: straight and harsh.

Colour: fawn to dark gray.

Characteristics Strong and hardy, the Picardy makes an effective guard, and has a good reputation with children. It requires firm and consistent early training and socialization to prevent overprotective instincts, plenty of exercise, moderate grooming.

PULI/HUNGARIAN PULI

History Like its cousin, the larger Komondor, this is a very ancient Hungarian sheepdog.

Appearance Short, compact and muscular in frame, it has a round head, distinct stop and straight muzzle. Ears, medium, pendant; eyes, dark; tail, may be naturally bobbed, otherwise long, curling.

Height: 37-44cm (14-18in).

Weight: 10-15kg (22-33lb).

Coat: corded, with long, coarse outer coat and dense inner.

Colour: black or gray.

Characteristics Hardy, active, and independent, this dog is normally an affectionate and gentle family dog, but it can be over-protective and needs to be firmly trained and socialized. Adapts well to most environments, but coat requires special care avoiding comb and brush. Moderate exercise.

BEARDED COLLIE

History Almost certainly descended from the Polish Sheepdog in the 15th century, it was developed in Scotland and known as the Highland Collie.

Appearance Deep-chested, strong and long in body, it has a broad head and long muzzle. Ears, medium, pendant; eyes, harmonize with coat; tail, slightly curved.

Height: 51-56cm (20-22in).

Weight: 18-27kg (40-60lb).

Coat: long, hard, straight outer, soft under, moustache, beard, brows.

Colour: includes black, shades of gray or sandy, with or withou white.

Characteristics Fun-loving, friendly, intelligent, makes a good family pet. Requires long walks and careful grooming to keep coat tangle-free.

POLISH LOWLAND SHEEPDOG/ POLSKI OWCZAREK NIZINNY/ VALÉE SHEEPDOG

History This intelligent, hard-working herder and guard has a long history in Poland dating back to Phoenician times.
Appearance A strong, stocky dog, it has a longish body and a largish, well-proportioned head with strong jaws. Ears, medium length, triangular; eyes, brown; tail, naturally short, or docked.
Height: 40-52cm (16-20in).
Weight: 29kg (63lb).
Coat: weather-resistant, long, heavy, straight.
Colour: all permissable.
Characteristics Hardy, intelligent, friendly, it makes a good house and family dog, but needs to be consistently trained and given plenty of exercise. Requires considerable grooming.

OLD ENGLISH SHEEPDOG/BOBTAIL

History Known in England for 200 years, its origins are unknown. It was highly regarded as a guard and herder of cattle and sheep.
Appearance Large, compact, and muscular it has a distinctive ambling gait, broad head and long, strong jaws. Ears, small, pendant; eyes, dark; tail, either naturally bobbed, more commonly docked.
Height: 56cm (22in). *Weight:* 30kg (66lb).
Coat: long, profuse, shaggy.
Colour: blue-gray to grizzle, usually with white markings.
Characteristics Hardy, agile and strong, it has an affectionate, playful, but biddable nature. A good family dog, it requires firm training, moderate exercise, but time-consuming coat care; some owners trim coat if the dog is not shown.

WELSH CORGIS: CARDIGAN AND PEMBROKE (RIGHT)

KOMONDOR

History An old Hungarian breed, recorded as far back as the 16th century, it is related to the Puli and was used on farms to protect herds against predators such as wolves which it could kill.

Appearance Large and powerful it has a broad head and muzzle. Ears, medium length, pendant; eyes, dark; tail, slightly curved.

Height: 59-66cm (23^1/$_2$-26in).

Weight: 59kg (125lb).

Coat: corded with long coarse outer, and soft under.

Colour: white.

Characteristics Courageous, strong, affectionate, it is easily trained and makes a good companion and family dog. It needs space, moderate exercise and time-consuming care of coat that can be trimmed, but not combed or brushed.

History The origin of both these little working dogs is unrecorded, but the type is known to have existed for a long time, possibly arriving in the British Isles with the Celts. Used mainly as cattle dogs, moving swiftly in and out at heel level, hence their local name of Welsh Heeler, the two distinct breeds were defined in 1925.

Appearance These little dogs are deep-chested, sturdy, low in body and short-legged, and have fox-like heads. Ears, quite large and erect (more pointed in the Pembroke); eyes, brown; tail, quite long, brush-like on the Cardigan, but the Pembroke has either a naturally short tail, or it is commonly docked.

Height: of Cardigan: 25-30cm (10-12in) – the Pembroke is slightly smaller.

Weight: 10-12.5kg (22-28lb).

Colour: the Cardigan is any colour or mixture except predominantly white; the Pembroke is fawn, red, sable, or black and tan, with or without white markings.

Characteristics Lively, hardy and intelligent, these dogs make good pets and companions, and effective watchdogs. The Pembroke has the rather more outgoing character. Both varieties need to be well exercised to keep in shape, and regularly groomed.

CANAAN DOG

History Well established in Israel, this Middle Eastern dog is descended from Pariah dogs and is used to guard property and herds.

Appearance It has a strong, well-proportioned, rather light frame, and a neat head with quite a deep muzzle. Ears, small, erect; eyes, brown; tail, has high, open curve.

Height: 50-61cm (20-24in).

Weight: 18-25kg (40-55lb).

Coat: medium length, straight, dense, harsh, weather resistant undercoat, some feathering.

Colour: sandy to reddish brown, white with red, brown or black markings.

Characteristics Even-tempered, intelligent and obedient, it is

used as a guide for the blind, for mine-detecting, finding war wounded, and as a popular companion, family dog and guard. It needs moderate exercise, minimum grooming, but tendency to bark should be controlled when young.

LANCASHIRE HEELER

History The origins of this little cattle dog are lost in history, but it is likely to have both Corgi and old Manchester Black and Tan Terrier in its make up.

Appearance Short-legged, and strong like the Corgis, it has a fox-like head. Ears, semi- or fully erect; eyes, brown; tail, slightly curved.

Height: 25-30cm (10-12in).
Weight: 10-12kg (22-26lb).
Coat: fairly short and sleek.
Colour: black with tan markings.
Characteristics Combining both terrier and herding talents, this is an independent, sometimes rather pugnacious little character requiring firm discipline from an early age, plenty of exercise, minimum grooming.

SWEDISH VALLHUND/SWEDISH CATTLE DOG/VASGOTASPETS

History This type of small dog, similar in looks to the Corgi, and probably crossed with Corgis by the Vikings, has been known in Sweden for more than 1,000 years, and used as a cattle dog and watchdog.

Appearance Short-legged, compact and muscular (higher off the ground than the Corgi), it has a flatish head and pointed muzzle. Ears, short, erect, pointed; eyes, dark; tail, short.

Height: 33-40cm (13-16in).
Weight: 9-14kg (20-31lb).
Coat: fairly short, hard, thick with weather-resistant undercoat.
Colour: grizzled, shades of gray, brownish yellow to red.
Characteristics Active, loyal, courageous, friendly and intelligent, this is a good family dog, often rather protective. Better adapted to country life than town requiring regular exercise, but minimum grooming.

Other Working and
Utility Dogs

MASTIFF/OLD ENGLISH MASTIFF

History Although its distant origins are obscure, this dog was well-known in Britain in Roman times and much admired for its feats in battle.

Appearance Very large, heavy, and well set, it has a broad head and short, strong muzzle. Ears, small, lie flat; eyes hazel to dark; tail, slightly curved.

Height: 70-75cm (27$^1/_2$-30in).

Weight: 79-86kg (175-190lb).

Coat: short and close.

Colour: apricot, silver, fawn, dark fawn, or brindle.

Characteristics Intelligent, friendly, quiet and sociable, it makes a loyal and successful family dog for those with space. Protective instincts only aroused if threat perceived on its family. Requires consistent early training, moderate exercise, minimum grooming.

NEAPOLITAN MASTIFF

History Making an interesting comparison with the (English) Mastiff, it has an equally long history in southern Italy where it was used in battle, as a fighter, as a draft animal and for police work.

Appearance Large and powerful, it has a broad head with long dewlaps. Ears, naturally semi-erect, cropped in some countries; eyes, light to brown; tail, often docked by one third.

Height: 60-75cm (24-30in).

Weight: 70kg (155lb).

Coat: short, close, shiny.

Colour: dark-lead, gray, fawn, or brindle, occasionally white markings.

Characteristics Peaceful, affectionate, obedient, it is a sound family dog provided it is well-trained, properly exercised and given the space its size demands.

NEWFOUNDLAND

History This big, water-loving dog has existed in Newfoundland for two centuries or more, though its ancestry remains uncertain. The LANDSEER is a colour variation of the same dog.

Appearance Large and strong, it has a broad, rounded head and shortish, square muzzle. Ears, small, pendant; eyes, dark; tail, slightly curved.

Height: 65-70cm (26-28in).
Weight: 50-68kg (110-150lb).
Coat: oily, long, flat, dense and coarse, with feathering.
Colour: black or brown, occasional tinges of bronze or white; Landseer is white and black.

Characteristics Docile, patient, good with children, these are fine family dogs for those who can provide the right environment – plenty of food, space and exercise. They require only moderate grooming.

GREAT DANE/DEUTSCHE DOGGE

History An ancient breed, coveted throughout Europe in the Middle Ages, it was developed in Germany and was highly regarded in noble households as both hunter and protector.

Appearance Large, noble and muscular in appearance, it has a clean, broad, long head. Ears, small, folded, cropped in some countries; eyes, dark (or harmonizing with coat); tail, tapering with slight curve.

Height: 71-76cm (28-30in).
Weight: 60kg (132lb).
Coat: short, dense and close.
Colour: brindle, fawn, blue, black, or harlequin.

Characteristics Affectionate and patient, it makes a gentle family dog, requiring firm early training, feeding and exercise commensurate with its size, and minimum grooming.

BULLMASTIFF

History Recognized as a breed in Britain in 1924, Bulldog-Mastiff crosses were used for protection work for a century or two earlier.

Appearance Has a powerful, well-proportioned frame, with a large, square head, well-defined stop and broad jaws. Ears, V-shaped, folded; eyes, hazel or dark, set wide with furrow between; tail, tapers.

Height: 61-68.5cm (24-27in).
Weight: 45-58kg (100-130lb).
Coat: short and hard.
Colour: fawn, red, or clear brindle.
Characteristics Reliable and sociable, it makes a friendly, obedient family dog. Requires early discipline to check exuberance, plenty of exercise, and minimum grooming.

LEONBERGER

History Although it has proved a fine water rescue dog, this breed was developed more for its appearance than usefulness in the 19th century in Germany from Newfoundlands, Great Pyrenees and St Bernards.

Appearance Large, heavy and well-proportioned, it has a good head and strong jaws. Ears, oval, pendant; eyes, brown; tail, slightly curved; feet, webbed.
Height: 65-80cm (26-32in).

Weight: 40kg (88lb).
Coat: fairly long, soft, wavy, waterproof, with mane and feathering.
Colour: silver-gray, yellow, or reddish-brown, with dark masking and shading.
Characteristics Lively, affectionate, obedient and good with children, it makes a good family pet requiring consistent early training, plenty of exercise, and moderate grooming.

HOVAWART

History Dating back to the 14th century or before, this farmworker and guard virtually disappeared until redeveloped in Germany in the early 20th century.

Appearance This large, elegant dog has a broad head with longish muzzle. Ears, medium length, pendant; eyes, brown to dark; tail, carried low.

Height: 55-70cm (22-28in).

Weight: 25-40kg (55-88lb).

Coat: long, thick, wavy, with feathering.

Colour: black, gold, or black with gold markings.

Characteristics Intelligent, lively, affectionate and hardy, it makes a good family dog, but needs consistent training to control exuberance, plenty of space for exercise, moderate grooming.

BOXER

History Its origins are unknown, but it emerged as a type in the late 19th century in Germany where it was used for guard work.

Appearance Deep-chested with a square, muscular frame, it has a strong head with deep stop and short muzzle, sometimes undershot. Ears, small, folded, cropped in some countries; eyes, dark brown; tail, commonly docked short.

Height: 53-63cm (21-25in).

Weight: 24-32kg (53-71lb).

Coat: short, smooth, shiny.

Colour: brindle or fawn of various shades with white markings.

Characteristics Lively, boisterous and affectionate, it makes a good family dog needing firm, early discipline, plenty of vigorous exercise, and minimum grooming.

BULLDOG/ENGLISH BULLDOG

History Developed in Britain in the 13th century from the Mastiff specifically for bull-baiting – long since illegal – it is said to typify the British character.

Appearance Broad-chested, narrowing at the loins, it is very muscular and stocky with rather bowed look to front legs. Its head is very large and wrinkled with a squashed look to the upturned, undershot lower jaw. Ears, small, folded; eyes, wide apart, dark brown; tail, tapers.

Height: 30-35cm (12-14in).

Weight: 22-25kg (49-55lb).
Coat: fine, short and close.
Colour: fawn, red, brindle with or without white, white, and pied.
Characteristics Loyal, good-natured with children and gentle, it makes a good companion. Can be unpredictable with other animals if not disciplined early. It requires gentle exercise and minimum grooming. Puppies should be selected carefully to avoid over-exaggerations in form.

ROTTWEILER

History This powerful cattle-droving dog came into Central Europe with the Roman legions and got its name from the German town of Rottweil.

Appearance This large, compact, strong dog, has a fine broad head and deep muzzle. Ears, smallish, pendant; eyes, dark; tail, commonly docked.

Height: 58.5-68.5cm (23-27in).
Weight: 50kg (110lb).
Coat: short, dense, flat.
Colour: black with tan markings.
Characteristics Fearless, loyal, powerful, it requires firm training, plentiful exercise, but minimum grooming. Strongly territorial if threat to owner or property is perceived. Puppies must be bought carefully.

DALMATIAN

History This old European breed is most likely to have descended mainly from Pointers. Its appearance gave it considerable fashion status in the 19th century when it used to run alongside or between the wheels of carriages.

Appearance It has a clean, symmetrical, muscular frame with a longish head and jaws and moderate stop. Ears, medium length, pendant; eyes, dark or amber; tail, tapering with slight curve.

Height: 56-60cm (22-24in).
Weight: 25kg (55lb).
Coat: short, hard, dense and glossy.
Colour: black or liver spots on white.

Characteristics Lively and cheerful, it makes a good family dog, requiring extensive exercise, plenty of companionship, minimum grooming.

FRENCH BULLDOG

History Likely to have evolved from small varieties of Bulldog, this breed was developed in France and was very popular in the 19th century.

Appearance Compact, barrel-chested and muscular, it has a broad, square head with short, square jaws. Ears, bat-like, erect; eyes, dark, round; tail, naturally short either kinked or straight, docked in some countries.

Height: 30cm (12in).
Weight: 9-12kg (20-28lb).
Coat: fine, close, smooth.
Colour: brindle, pied, or fawn.

Characteristics Affectionate, active and intelligent, it thrives on constant companionship and games, and makes a good companion. It needs moderate exercise, minimum grooming, but controlled diet to avoid problems of overweight.

SHAR-PEI/CHINESE FIGHTING DOG

History Originating from China where it was bred to fight, it is unusual like the Chow Chow in that it has a black-purple tongue.
Appearance Sturdy and muscular in body, its skin is loose and heavily folded. Its head is square, very wrinkled and broad. Ears, tiny, folded; eyes, small, deepset, brown; tail, curves high.
Height: 41-51cm (16-20in).
Weight: 16-25kg (35-55lb).
Coat: short and bristly.
Colour: fawn, cream, red, black.
Characteristics Quiet-natured and loyal, this dog can make a good companion requiring firm training and socialization when young, moderate exercise, and minimum grooming. Puppies must be carefully checked.

BOSTON TERRIER

History An American breed, developed from Bulldog, Boxer, and Terrier crosses, it was first shown in 1870.
Appearance Short and deep in body, it has a broad, flat head and short, square muzzle, sometimes slightly undershot jaw. Ears, bat-like, erect, in some countries cropped; eyes, dark, large, round; tail, naturally short and tapering straight or screw.

Height: 38-43cm (15-17in).
Weight: 7-11kg (15-25lb) – it is classed by weight.
Coat: short, fine, shiny.
Colour: brindle, occasionally black, with white markings.
Characteristics Playful, intelligent and obedient, it is good-natured with children making a popular pet needing only moderate exercise and minimum grooming.

93

Miniature

Toy

Standard

POODLES: STANDARD, MINIATURE, TOY

History The three sizes of Poodle all originate from the same source, the smaller varieties having been selectively bred down. They almost certainly owe their distinctive coat to the old Water Dog of Germany, and the old French Barbet is also claimed as a Poodle ancestor. Bred as gundogs, the Standard was an effective retriever in and out of water, but as natural performers, they then became much better known as clever circus dogs, before the Miniature and Toy achieved the status of being perhaps the most popular of all companion dogs.

Appearance Deep-chested and compact in frame, they have long, fine-muzzled heads held high. Ears long, pendant; eyes, dark brown; tails, commonly docked.

Height: Standard – over 38cm (15in); Miniature – 28-37cm (11-14$\frac{1}{2}$in); Toy – under 28cm (11in).

Weight: Standard – 22kg (49lb); Miniature – 12kg (26lb); Toy – 7kg (15lb).

Coat: curly, corded, does not shed.

Colour: all solid colours.

Characteristics Neat in action, these friendly, intelligent dogs are easily trained and make good family pets, being adaptable, and requiring only moderate exercise. Their coats, however, require time-consuming attention, and some trimming to keep them under control. Ears need regular checks.

Minature

andard

Giant

HNAUZERS: GIANT, STANDARD, MINIATURE

story This type of dog is recorded as far back as the 16th century
southern German farming areas, and contains a good proportion
terrier as well as working blood in its make up. The Giant
obably owes its size to Briard or Bouvier des Flandres influence,
: Standard to Pinschers, and the Miniature to Affenpinschers.
ey are all courageous guards, but it is the Miniature that has the
eatest popularity as a family pet.

pearance Square, muscular dogs with upright carriage, they have
her long heads and strong jaws. Ears, naturally folded, in some
untries cropped; eyes, dark; tail, commonly docked.

ight: Giant – 60-70cm (23$^{1}/_{2}$-27$^{1}/_{2}$in); Standard – 46-48cm (18-
n); Miniature – 33-35cm (13-14in).

ight: Giant – 35kg (77lb); Standard – 15kg (33lb); Miniature –
kg (14lb).

at: medium length, thick, coarse, and hard, with distinct brows,
ustache and beard.

lour: black, or pepper and salt.

aracteristics Hardy, lively and loyal, the Giant is still very much
vorking, country dog, while the Standard and Miniature adapt well
most environments. The Miniature is friendly and patient with
ildren, but all have quick terrier responses and the two smaller
rieties can be barkers. They need plentiful exercise proportionate
their sizes, and minimum grooming, but benefit from stripping.

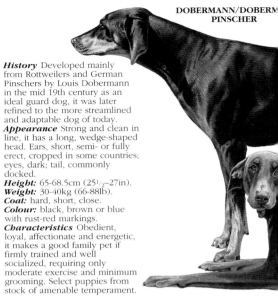

DOBERMANN/DOBERM
PINSCHER

History Developed mainly from Rottweilers and German Pinschers by Louis Dobermann in the mid 19th century as an ideal guard dog, it was later refined to the more streamlined and adaptable dog of today.

Appearance Strong and clean in line, it has a long, wedge-shaped head. Ears, short, semi- or fully erect, cropped in some countries; eyes, dark; tail, commonly docked.

Height: 65-68.5cm (25½–27in).
Weight: 30-40kg (66-88lb).
Coat: hard, short, close.
Colour: black, brown or blue with rust-red markings.

Characteristics Obedient, loyal, affectionate and energetic, it makes a good family pet if firmly trained and well socialized, requiring only moderate exercise and minimum grooming. Select puppies from stock of amenable temperament.

GERMAN PINSCHER

History Probably descended from medieval hunting dogs, this breed has been known in Germany for many centuries before official recognition at the end of the 19th century.

Appearance Lithe and compact in body, it has a long narrow head and muzzle. Ears, naturally semi-erect, cropped in some countries; eyes, dark; tail commonly, docked.

Height: 45-58cm (18-19in).
Weight: 6-8kg (13-18lb).
Coat: short, close and shiny.

Colour: black, chestnut, red, or blue-gray with markings, or pepper and salt.

Characteristics Sporty, intelligent and biddable, it make a good family and house dog, though over-inclined to bark. A natural hunter of vermin, it requires firm discipline, moderat exercise and minimum groomin

The HARLEQUIN PINSCHER with its distinctive spotty markings, is a little smaller and, although it has a good reputatio as a family dog, is rarely seen.

PORTUGUESE WATER DOG
History Bred by Portuguese
fishermen for centuries to
retrieve escaping fish, catch
ropes, rescue and guard.
Appearance A strongly built
dog, both long- and short-coat
varieties are the same. The head
is well-proportioned and quite
large with noticeable stop. Ears,
triangular, pendant; eyes, dark;
feet webbed; tail, curves up and
over the back.
Height: 43-57cm (17-22in).
Weight: 16-25kg (35-55lb).
Coat: for the long-coat variety is
thick, strong and wavy; the short-
coat variety has shorter, more
curly hair.
Colour: black, white, or
chestnut, and mixtures.
Characteristics Adaptable to
most environments, it is a
watchful, faithful companion, can
be pugnacious and is a powerful
swimmer. Needs to be kept
active and well exercised and the
substantial coat needs care and
trimming; a special clip reflecting
its swimming work is used for
showing.

AUSTRIAN PINSCHER/AUSTRIAN SHORTHAIRED PINSCHER
History An old Austrian breed,
has decided terrier attributes
being a vigilant watch dog and
quick to despatch vermin.
Appearance A broader, sturdier
dog than its German cousin, it
has a pear-shaped head. Ears,
neat, fold forward; eyes, brown;
tail, curves over back, or docked.
Height: 35-50cm (14-20in).
Weight: 12-18kg (26-40lb).

Coat: short, strong.
Colour: yellow, fawn, red,
reddish-black, with white
markings.
Characteristics Alert, bright,
quick, it is amenable to training
and makes an excellent watch
and house dog. Its fast responses
require supervision when with
young children. Needs plentiful
exercise, minimum grooming.

97

SHIH TZU/CHRYSANTHEMUM DOG
History Brought to the Imperial palace in China from Tibet centuries ago, it was known as the Lion Dog and kept as a palace guard and favoured pet.
Appearance Quite heavy for its size, it has a long, sturdy, little body and a round, broad head with short square muzzle. Ears, long pendant; eyes, quite large, dark brown; tail curls over high on the back.
Height: 26.5cm (10¹/₂in).
Weight: 4.5-7kg (10-16lb).
Coat: long, strong, straight and thick, with moustache and beard.
Colour: all colours.
Characteristics Hardy, lively, good-natured with children, and rather independent, it makes an adaptable pet requiring moderate exercise and regular attention to coat.

TIBETAN TERRIER
History Originating in Japan, this dog accompanied caravans to China as a valued and vociferous herder and watch dog.
Appearance Strong, compact, it has a medium length head and muzzle. Ears, medium length, pendant; eyes, dark; tail, curls over back.
Height: 35.5-40.5cm (14-16in).
Weight: 6.8kg (15lb).
Coat: profuse, fine, slightly wavy outer, fine, woolly under, and long brows, moustache, beard and feathering.
Colour: all colours except chocolate.
Characteristics Hardy, intelligent, gentle and adaptable, it is a popular pet with an unusually deep bark. It needs moderate exercise, but time spent on grooming.

98

LHASA APSO/TIBETAN APSO

History This very ancient Tibetan breed was kept and revered in the monasteries as both a symbol of good fortune and an effective little watch dog.
Appearance Has a long, sturdy frame with longish head and muzzle. Ears, long, pendant; eyes, dark; tail, curls over.
Height: 25.5cm (10in).
Weight: 5.9-6.8kg (13-15lb).
Coat: long, coarse outer coat and dense inner, with heavy feathering, moustache and beard.
Colour: sandy-gold, dark grizzle, slate gray, brown, black, white and particolour.
Characteristics This independent little dog repays plentiful attention with devoted friendship and needs only moderate exercise but regular grooming to keep coat in condition.

TIBETAN SPANIEL

History For several centuries this little Tibetan dog was kept as a favoured pet in the monasteries and was used to turn the prayer wheels. It is a likely ancestor of the Pekingese which it resembles in some features.
Appearance Quite a strong, well-proportioned dog, it has a slightly domed head, slight stop and medium length, blunt muzzle. Ears, medium length, pendant; eyes, dark; tail, curls over back when alert.
Height: 25.5cm (10in).
Weight: 4.1-6.8kg (9-15lb).
Coat: medium length, silky outer coat, close under, with feathering.
Colour: all colours and mixtures.
Characteristics Cautious of strangers, this is an alert, affectionate dog making a good family pet requiring only moderate grooming and exercise.

Terriers

AIREDALE TERRIER

History Bred in Yorkshire in the mid 19th century to hunt badger and otter, it is the largest of the terrier group and has the Otterhound and the old Black and Tan Terrier in its make-up.

Appearance It is a deep-chested, strong, well-proportioned dog with long head and muzzle. Ears, small, v-shaped, fall forward; eyes brown; tail, medium length, carried up.

Height: 56-61cm (22-24in).

Weight: 20kg (44lb).

Coat: dense, wiry outer coat, shorter soft under.

Colour: tan with black or grizzle markings.

Characteristics Lively and good-natured, it is a loyal family dog, but its keen hunting instincts require firm discipline. It needs plenty of exercise, but only minimum grooming.

BEDLINGTON TERRIER

History This unlikely-looking terrier goes back to the Border counties of England and Scotland in the early 19th century and owes its appearance to Whippet and Dandie Dinmont crossings with other terrier types to produce the speed to catch rabbits and the strength to deal with vermin.

Appearance It has an arching back, a lithe, muscular frame, and a pear-shaped head. Ears, medium length, pendant; eyes, hazel to dark; tail, tapering and curved.

Height: 38-43cm (15-17in).

Weight: 8-10kg (18-23lb).

Coat: dense, twisty, and fairly soft.

Colour: blue, blue and tan, liver, or sandy.

Characteristics Neat and friendly, it remains a fast, keen hunter preferring hard country to apartment life, but will adapt to most environments if given plenty of mental stimulus and moderate exercise. Its coat needs regular grooming and trimming.

WELSH TERRIER

History Originating from old wirehaired, black and tan terriers, the Welsh was developed over generations in Wales to hunt vermin, badger, fox, and otter.
Appearance Quite long-legged, but compact and muscular, it has a longish, flat head and strong jaws. Ears, v-shaped, fall forward; eyes, dark; tail, erect, commonly partially docked.
Height: 40cm (15$\frac{1}{2}$in).

Weight: 9kg (20lb).
Coat: double, wiry, abundant and close.
Colour: black and tan, or black grizzle and tan.
Characteristics Hardy, lively and affectionate, it is easily trained and adaptable, making a good family dog. It requires regular exercise, moderate grooming, some trimming.

SOFT-COATED WHEATEN TERRIER

History This breed, originating in County Kerry, Ireland, certainly goes back several centuries, but was only recognized in Ireland in 1937. An effective controller of vermin, it was also used to herd, retrieve and as a guard.
Appearance A strong dog, compact and well-balanced, it has a fairly long head, definite stop and strong jaws. Ears, v-shaped, folded; eyes, dark; tail,

commonly docked.
Height: 43-49cm (17-19$\frac{1}{2}$in).
Weight: 15.8-18kg (35-40lb).
Coat: long, abundant, silky and wavy or curly.
Colour: wheaten.
Characteristics Hardy, sporting and gentle, it is adaptable to most environments, but needs firm training to control over-exuberance and plenty of exercise. Its coat needs very regular, careful grooming.

101

SMOOTH FOX TERRIER AND WIRE FOX TERRIER

History These terriers were used to run with hounds in the early 19th century, and by introducing the old wirehaired and old English white terriers, the smooth and wire varieties were produced.

Appearance Built for quick action, they have deep-chested, short-backed bodies, and long, lean, heads with tapering muzzles. Ears, small, fold forward; eyes, dark; tails, commonly docked.

Height: 37-39cm (14½-15½in).

Weight: 8kg (18lb).

Coat: short, dense and hard for Smooth; dense, wiry outer with softer under coat for the Wire.

Colour: white with markings of most colours, though not brindle.

Characteristics Active and intelligent, these adaptable dogs make affectionate family dogs, though they need to be well trained and properly exercised to control hunting instincts. The Wire requires more intensive coat care and benefits from trimming.

LAKELAND TERRIER

History Developed from several of the northern English terrier breeds to cope with the wild terrain of the Lake District, the breed club was formed in 1912.

Appearance Square, agile and muscular, it has a flatish, well-proportioned head with fairly broad muzzle. Ears, quite small, v-shaped, drop forward; eyes, hazel to dark; tail, short and upright.

Height: 36.5cm (14½in).

Weight: 6.8-7.7kg (15-17lb).

Coat: double, thick and harsh.

Colour: red, wheaten, red grizzle, blue, or black, or black or blue and tan.

Characteristics Adaptable, playful, and friendly, it makes a good companion and family dog requiring moderate exercise, regular grooming, and benefitting from occasional trimming.

KERRY BLUE TERRIER

History This large Irish terrier was developed in the remote valleys of Kerry to combine the qualities of hunter, retriever on land and water, and guard.

Appearance This is a powerful, compact dog with long, lean head and strong jaws. Ears, v-shaped, drop forward; eyes, dark; tail, commonly docked.

Height: 43-48cm (17-19in).

Weight: 16kg (35lb).

Coat: thick, soft, silky and wavy.

Colour: silver to steel blue. (Adult colour not distinguishable until over 18 months.)

Characteristics An adaptable, good-natured house and family dog, it is capable of aggression and stubbornness but will respond well to firm training and early socialization. It requires only moderate exercise, but a fair measure of regular grooming and some trimming.

IRISH TERRIER

History Originating from old wirehaired terriers, but only recognized in the late 19th century, it is distinguished by its racy lines that give it wide-ranging hunting abilities.

Appearance Tall, lithe and well-proportioned, it has a longish, flat head and long muzzle. Ears, v-shaped, fall forward; eyes, dark; tail, commonly partially docked.

Height: 46cm (18in).

Weight: 11.3-12.3kg (25-27lb).

Coat: double, hard, coarse and wavy.

Colour: wheaten gold.

Characteristics Good-natured, adaptable and easily trained, it makes a good family and house dog requiring moderate exercise, minimum grooming, but regular stripping.

103

BORDER TERRIER

History Bred in the late 19th century in the British Border countrie
to run with Foxhounds and follow quarry to earth.

Appearance It has longish, fairly narrow but sturdy body and
moderately broad head with strong otter-muzzle. Ears, small,
v-shaped, drop forward; eyes, dark; tail, fairly short and straight.

Height: 25cm (10in).

Weight: 5-7kg (11½-15½lb).

Coat: short, hard, dense outer coat, close under.

Colour: tan, blue and tan, grizzle and tan, wheaten, or red.

Characteristics Hardy, energetic, intelligent and generous-natured
it adapts well to most environments and family life. Inclined to be
stubborn, it needs firm early discipline as well as plentiful exercise,
though only moderate grooming.

104

MANCHESTER TERRIER
History Bred in Manchester from the centuries old Black and Tan Terrier and the Whippet to create a fast, doughty hunter of vermin, it was generally well-known by the end of the 19th century.
Appearance It has a well-proportioned, rather narrow, compact frame with longish, neat head and jaws. Ears, v-shaped, fold forward; eyes, hazel to dark; tail, slightly curved.
Height: 35.5-40.5cm (14-16in).
Weight: 5.4-9kg (12-20lb).
Coat: short, close and smooth.
Colour: black and tan.

Characteristics Well-adapted to human companionship, it is friendly with children, tidy in habit and makes a good pet, requiring moderate exercise and minimum grooming.

KROMFOHRLÄNDER
History This German breed is said to have been created after the Second World War from a litter produced by a Wirehaired Terrier and a dog abandoned by American troops. But others put its origins in the 19th century.
Appearance Well-proportioned and agile, it has a longish head and muzzle. Ears, short to medium length, fold forward; eyes, brown; tail, curves over.
Height: 39-46cm (15-18in).
Weight: 12kg (26lb).
Coat: variable length, rough and wiry, or short and coarse, with light feathering.
Colour: white with chestnut markings.
Characteristics Intelligent, faithful and friendly, it makes a good and adaptable family dog, only requiring moderate exercise and grooming.

The older JAGDTERRIER or German Hunting Terrier is a lean, tough little dog bred to work courageously, but not as a family pet.

PARSON JACK RUSSELL TERRIER
History Bred by the Rev'd Jack Russell in Devon in the early 19th century who sought to create a terrier capable of tackling a fox underground, it comes in many types, and the breed has only recently been formally recognized in Britain.
Appearance Sturdy, compact and muscular, it has a fairly broad head and strong jaws. Ears, small, v-shaped, fold forward; eyes, dark; tail, commonly docked.
Height: 33cm (13in).
Weight: 4.5kg (10lb).
Coat: rough or smooth, harsh, dense and close.
Colour: all hound colours.
Characteristics Courageous and lively, it makes a devoted pet, but needs firm handling to curb hunting instincts, plentiful exercise, minimum grooming.

CAIRN TERRIER

History Known for centuries on the Island of Skye and getting its name from the piles of stones (cairns) in which it was adept at raising a lurking fox, it was formally recognized in the early 20th century.

Appearance Compact and sturdy in body, it has a fairly broad head and strong jaws. Ears, small, erect; eyes, dark hazel; tail, naturally quite short.

Height: 23cm (9in).
Weight: 6.3kg (14lb).
Coat: shaggy, hard outer, soft, close under.
Colour: red, sandy, brindle, gray.
Characteristics Adaptable, lively and intelligent, it makes a bright companion requiring early discipline to control over-protectiveness and noisiness, moderate exercise, minimum grooming.

AUSTRALIAN TERRIER

History Developed in Australia towards the end of the 19th century from a variety of terrier crosses, it is an effective vermin hunter and watch dog.

Appearance Has a deep-chested, sturdy, low-set little frame and rather long head with slight stop. Ears, pointed, erect; eyes, dark brown; tail, commonly docked.

Height: 25.5cm (10in).
Weight: 4.5-5kg (10-11lb).
Coat: medium length, hard outer and softer undercoat, with brows, moustache and topknot.
Colour: blue with tan markings, or red.
Characteristics This hardy, lively, courageous little dog has very quick reactions. It makes an adaptable, intelligent pet, requiring only moderate exercise and grooming.

106

SKYE TERRIER

History One of the oldest Scottish terrier breeds, it dates back at least to Elizabethan times and was used to ferret out fox, badger and otter from their lairs.

Appearance It has a long, strong, low body and a longish head with strong jaws. Ears, either pricked or pendant; eyes, hazel to dark; tail, slightly curved.

Height: 23-25cm (9-10in).
Weight: 10-11.3kg (22-25lb).
Coat: long, hard outer coat, and soft, dense under.
Colour: any whole colour with shading of same colour, black nose and ears.

Characteristics Cautious of strangers, this active, friendly dog is loyal to its family and makes an intelligent companion. It enjoys strenuous exercise, and coat requires moderate grooming.

NORFOLK TERRIER AND NORWICH TERRIER

History These were bred in East Anglia from Irish, Border and Cairn Terriers in the mid 19th century to be short enough to penetrate fox and badger holes and strong enough to deal with them. The two breeds were recently separated in Britain and are distinguished from each other primarily by their ears.

Appearance Small, compact and strong, they have a slightly rounded head, well-defined stop, and wedge-shaped muzzle. Ears, short, fold forward in the Norfolk, erect in the Norwich; eyes, dark; tail, commonly docked short.

Height: 25cm (10in).
Weight: 4.5-5.4kg (10-12lb).
Coat: medium length, straight, wiry and hard, rougher around neck.
Colour: red, red-wheaten, black and tan, or grizzle.

Characteristics Hardy, fearless and friendly, they make good little watch dogs and adaptable pets requiring plenty of exercise, but minimum grooming.

WEST HIGHLAND WHITE TERRIER

History White Scottish terriers were originally more leggy than
now, being developed to hunt easily over rugged terrain. The breed
was first recognized in the mid 19th century.

Appearance Compact and sturdy, it has a slightly domed skull,
defined stop and strong jaws. Ears, small, pointed, erect; eyes, dark
brown; tail, quite short and straight.

Height: 28cm (11in). *Weight:* 7-10kg (15-22lb).

Coat: medium length, hard straight outer coat, with furry, soft under.

Colour: white.

Characteristics Hardy, brave, fun-loving and affectionate, it makes
a good family pet and house dog. It responds to plenty of attention,
as much exercise as it can get, regular grooming and some trimming.

SEALYHAM TERRIER

History Possibly dating back to,
the 15th century, the breed was
fully developed by a Captain
Edwards in the latter half of the
19th century.

Appearance Rather deep in
body and with very sturdy, short
legs, it has a rounded head with
a long square muzzle. Ears,
shortish, drop sideways; eyes,
round, dark; tail, upright.

Height: 25cm (10in).

Weight: 8.1-9kg (18-20lb).

Coat: double, with long, hard
and wiry outer.

Colour: white, or white with
light head markings.

Characteristics Hardy, cheerfu
and affectionate, it needs firm
training, plenty of exercise, and
careful grooming and trimming.

BOHEMIAN TERRIER/CZESKY TERRIER

History Containing Scottish Terrier and Sealyham in its make-up, this fairly modern dog was developed in Czechoslovakia to tackle both badger and fox underground.
Appearance It is short-legged, with a sturdy, long body, longish head and strong jaws. Ears, medium length, folded; eyes, brown; tail, slightly curved.
Height: 27-35cm (11-14in).
Weight: 6-9kg (13-20lb).

Coat: medium length, dense, slightly wavy, with feathering, beard and brows.
Colour: gray-blue or light coffee with lighter markings.
Characteristics A hardy, active, powerful little dog, it is protective of its family and adaptable to most environments requiring moderate exercise and grooming. Its coat is usually clipped.

SCOTTISH TERRIER/ABERDEEN TERRIER

History For centuries before the breed club was formed in 1882, there was a wide variety of local terriers called "Scottish" in the Aberdeen area of Scotland.
Appearance Short-legged and thick-set, this dog has a long, rather narrow head with slight stop and strong muzzle. Ears, pointed, erect; eyes, dark brown; tail, medium length, upright.
Height: 25-28cm (10-11in).
Weight: 8.6-10.4kg (19-23lb).
Coat: medium length, dense, wiry outer, dense, soft inner, weather-resistant, and beard.
Colour: black, wheaten, or brindle.
Characteristics Lively, intelligent, friendly to those it knows, it is a loyal family dog responding to firm, gentle discipline to control over-protectiveness. It requires moderate exercise, careful grooming and occasional trimming.

Terriers

BULL TERRIER

History Originally bred in the mid 19th century as a fighter from the Staffordshire Bull Terrier, the old English White Terrier and possibly Pointer and Dalmation, the dog we know today is a little more refined than its rough forebears.

Appearance The broad, deep chest and curving profile of the head are distinctive features of this sturdy, muscular dog. Ears, erect; eye narrow, dark; tail, strong, straight.

Height: 53-56cm (21-22in).

Weight: 23.5-28kg (52-62lb).

Coat: short, hard, smooth.

Colour: white, white with markings, or mainly coloured, often brindle.

Characteristics Proverbially gentle with and protective of children this neat, intelligent dog can respond powerfully to a perceived threat and needs to be well socialized, firmly trained, and well exercised. Requires minimum grooming.

The MINIATURE BULL TERRIER is identical in all respects except size 35.5cm (14in).

STAFFORDSHIRE BULL TERRIER

History The crossing of Bulldog with other terriers created a dogged fighter in the 19th century. When the practice of dog fighting was made illegal, the breed survived due to its character.

Appearance Agile and muscular, it has a broad, deep chest, and its head is wide with a definite stop, round cheeks, and powerful jaws. Ears, small, semi-erect; eyes, dark brown; tail, pump-handle shaped.

Height: 35.5-40.5cm (14-16in).

Weight: 10.8-17kg (24-38lb).

Coat: close, smooth, short.

Colour: includes red, fawn, or brindle with or without white markings.

Characteristics Devotion to children and friendly loyalty to their human family are the hallmarks of this strong, agile dog. It requires firm early training and socialization, plenty of exercise, but minimum grooming.

The AMERICAN STAFFORDSHIRE TERRIER (top left) was bred, like its smaller English cousin, as a fighting dog in the 19th century in the USA. Large and very muscular, its ears are semi-erect, in some countries docked. Courageous and generally friendly with humans, it can be very protective and aggressive to other dogs. Requires firm, consistent obedience training, moderate exercise, and minimum grooming. Puppies should be bought from reputable stock.

DANDIE DINMONT TERRIER

History This doughty hunter of badger, otter and fox emerged in the early 17th century, but acquired its name from a fictional character in Walter Scott's *Guy Mannering*.

Appearance Its gently arched, strong, long body has slightly shorter legs in front, and its head is large and domed with strong jaws. Ears, pendant; eyes, hazel; tail, short to medium.

Height: 20-28cm (8-11in).

Weight: 9kg (20lb).

Coat: medium length and double, combining hard and soft.

Colour: dark to light pepper-gray, or pale fawn to reddish, mustard-brown, with white.

Characteristics Independent, intelligent and quiet with children, it makes a good family and house dog, but needs firm training, moderate exercise, and careful, regular grooming.

111

Spitz and Nordic Dogs

SIBERIAN HUSKY/ARCTIC HUSKY

History Similar to the Malamute, but generally a faster hauler of sledges, it originated in Siberia where the type had been used for centuries.

Appearance Graceful and strong, it has a rounded, tapering head, defined stop, medium length muzzle. Ears, erect with slightly rounded tips; eyes, brown or blue; tail, carried up and over except when working.

Height: 51-60cm (20-23½in).

Weight: 16-27kg (35-60lb).

Coat: dense, straight outer, and soft, abundant inner (shed in spring).

Colour: all colours from black white with markings.

Characteristics Very hardy, friendly and intelligent, it is goo with children and reasonably adaptable. It prefers extensive exercise, and coat requires moderate grooming – more when moulting.

NORWEGIAN BUHUND

History Buhund means cattle dog which is what this dog wa bred in Norway to be. Its long history may date to the Middle Ages.

Appearance It has a strong, agile, compact body with wed shaped head and definite stop Ears, erect, pointed; eyes, dark brown; tail, curls over.

Height: 45cm (17½in).

Weight: 25kg (55lb).

Coat: thick, coarse outer, woo under, smooth on face and leg

Colour: wheaten, black, red, wolf-sable.

Characteristics Fearless, friendly, obedient and loyal, it also patient with children and makes a good family dog requiring regular, active exerc and moderate grooming.

ALASKAN MALAMUTE

History Named after the Inuit Mahlemut who used these dogs to haul sledges above the Arctic Circle, it is still one of the main sledge dogs in the North.
Appearance Large and powerful, it has a wedge-shaped head and strong muzzle. Ears, triangular, erect; eyes, brown; tail, loosely curled over.
Height: 58-63cm (23-25in).
Weight: 34-38kg (75-85lb).

Coat: thick, coarse outer and dense, oily, woolly under.
Colour: gray to black with distinctive white markings, or white.
Characteristics Very hardy, loyal and good-natured with humans, it can be aggressive to other dogs though will respond well to firm discipline. It requires plenty of exercise and hard grooming during moult.

NORWEGIAN ELKHOUND

History A very ancient Nordic hunting dog developed over centuries to scent, hunt, and put at bay the native Elk in snow and dense woodland.
Appearance Has a compact, strong and muscular body with broad head, moderate stop and tapering muzzle. Ears, erect, pointed; eyes, dark brown; tail, curls well over back.
Height: 49-52cm (19½-20½in).
Weight: 20-23kg (43-50lb).
Coat: abundant, coarse outer,

soft, woolly inner (shorter on head and legs) moulting in spring.
Colour: shades of gray.
Characteristics Hardy, adaptable, generous-natured, it makes a good, if large family dog requiring plenty of exercise and moderate grooming.

The JAMTHUND is a larger, more heavily built Swedish dog, similar to the Elkhound, and is a popular all-purpose dog in Sweden.

SAMOYED

History Taking its name from the nomadic Samoyed people of Siberia, who used it for herding reindeer, hauling, and as a companion, the Samoyed was introduced to England in 1889 with white soon becoming the popular colour.

Appearance A strong, active, sturdy dog, it has a broad wedge-shaped head and strong jaws. Ears, erect; eyes, medium to dark brown; tail, carried over the back.

Height: 48-60cm (19-23½in).
Weight: 23-30kg (50-65lb).
Coat: straight, harsh outer, with dense, soft under.
Colour: white, occasionally cream with light biscuit markings.
Characteristics Robust, lively affectionate, reliable and easily trained, it makes a popular family dog. It needs plenty of exercise and careful grooming particularly during moult.

FINNISH SPITZ

History This breed has existed for a long time in Finland and was probably developed from the Elkhound and Russian Laika.

Appearance Deep-chested, strong and square, it has a foxy-shaped head with deep stop. Ears, erect, pointed; eyes, dark; tail, curls up, over and down.

Height: 39-50cm (15½-20in).
Weight: 15-18kg (33-40lb).
Coat: medium length, stand-off outer, and soft, dense under, short on face and legs.

Colour: brown-red, or yellow-red, with lighter shadings.
Characteristics Hardy, brave, friendly with children, it makes loyal, if noisy family dog, requiring moderate exercise and grooming.

114

KARELIAN BEAR DOG/LAIKA

History Closely related to the Russian Laika, this breed was developed over centuries to hunt bear.

Appearance Strong and muscular, its head is wedge-shaped. Ears, pointed, erect; eyes, brown; tail, curls in circle.

Height: 54-60cm (21-24in).

Weight: 20-22kg (44-49lb).

Coat: thick, stand-off outer with dense inner.

Colour: black with white markings.

Characteristics Hardy and brave, it is essentially a one-man dog being naturally protective and fairly aggressive with other dogs. Careful breeding in recent years has improved its social manners. It requires firm control, plenty of exercise, moderate grooming.

GERMAN SPITZ: STANDARD (MITTEL) AND SMALL (KLEIN)

History Spitz dogs have been known in Germany since the beginning of the 17th century. Descended from the Nordic herding dogs, there are several varieties largely differentiated by height. The Small Spitz was the original Pomeranian, but is now distinct.

Appearance Deep-chested, strong and compact,they have well-proportioned, wedge-shaped heads with definite stop. Ears, erect; eyes, dark; tails, curl over.

Height: Standard: 29-35cm (11½-14in). Small: 23-28cm (9-11in).

Weight: Standard: 12kg (25lb). Small: 3.75kg (8lb).

Coat: medium length, abundant outer, soft under, smooth on face, feathering.

Colour: silvery-gray with black shading (wolf), black, white, orange, or deep brown.

Characteristics Active, intelligent, quite protective, and good with children, these are popular family dogs requiring moderate exercise but thorough grooming.

The largest of the German Spitz dogs is the WOLFSPITZ, which is only wolf-gray in colour; an equally popular family dog is the GRAND or GIANT (*Grossspitz*) at over 40cm (16in); and the little TOY (*Zwergspitz*) is under 22cm (8½in).

115

CHOW CHOW

History At least 2,000 years old, the "lion dog" was used as a hunter and guard in China, and it is a sad fact that breeding farms also existed to supply both skins and meat.

Appearance Has a rather stilted gait, and compact, sturdy body with a large, broad head and muzzle. Ears, small, erect; eyes, dark; tail, curls well over.

Height: 48-60cm (19-20in).

Weight: 24-27kg (55-60lb).

Coat: very abundant, stand-off, coarse outer, and soft, woolly inner.

Colour: black, red, blue, fawn, cream or white. Inside of mouth and tongue black.

Characteristics Its rather aloof expression belies an affectionate if rather temperamental character. It requires patient handling and leash-training, moderate exercise and regular grooming.

SCHIPPERKE

History The size of this dog can vary from very small to medium. It originally appeared in Belgium and Holland as a watch dog on the barges and was recognized as a breed in the late 19th century.

Appearance Compact and sturdy, it has a fox-like head. Ears, triangular, erect; eyes, dark brown; tail, either naturally without, or docked.

Height: 25-33cm (10-13in).

Weight: 5.5-8kg (12-18lb).

Coat: dense, harsh, with longer mane.

Colour: black most common, but also other solid colours.

Characteristics Active, intelligent, inquisitive and independent, it rewards firm training with lively companionship and loyalty, requiring only moderate exercise and minimum grooming.

116

VOLPINO ITALIANO/ FLORENTINE SPITZ

History This little dog – not common today – goes back to Roman times, and it was used for centuries as a vociferous guard on the farms and in the vineyards of Tuscany.

Appearance Sturdy and compact, it has a robust head, defined stop and strong jaws. Ears, triangular, erect; eyes, brown; tail, curls over.

Height: 25-30cm (10-12in).

Weight: 4kg (9lb).

Coat: long, abundant and thick, close on face and feet.

Colour: white or red.

Characteristics Hardy, lively, affectionate and adaptable, though inclined to be noisy, it makes a good family dog requiring moderate exercise and grooming.

The NORBOTTENSPETZ or small Nordic Spitz, usually white with red markings, has a fairly short coat. Recently revived, it is gaining in popularity.

EESHOND

istory Known for at least 200 ears as a guard and companion r the bargees in Holland, it robably owes part of its ncestry to the German Spitz. It claimed that it owes its name the Dutch patriot, Kees de yselaer.

ppearance Compact and uscular, it has a wedge-shaped ead, defined stop and moderate ngth muzzle. Ears, erect; eyes, ark; tail, curls over.

Height: 44-46cm (17-18in).

Weight: 25-30kg (55-66lb).

Coat: hard, stand-off outer, dense, soft inner, substantial ruff.

Colour: wolf-gray mixtures with "spectacles".

Characteristics Hardy, adaptable and intelligent, it makes a good house dog needing firm training to calm exuberance and barking, also requires plentiful exercise, moderate grooming.

117

JAPANESE SPITZ

History Probably taking its colour from the German or Nordic Spitz, this little Japanese lapdog is fast gaining worldwide popularity.

Appearance Has a compact, sturdy body and well-proportioned head and strong jaws. Ears, erect, pointed; eyes, dark; tail, curls over.

Height: 25-40cm (10-16in).
Weight: 10kg (22lb).
Coat: thick, medium length, shorter on face.
Colour: white.
Characteristics Hardy, active, intelligent and affectionate it makes a good family dog requiring moderate exercise and grooming.

JAPANESE AKITA/AKITA/ AKITA INU

History Developed in Japan in the early part of the 17th century to hunt bear and wild boar, it became the most important dog in that country being revered for its fine character and loyalty.

Appearance It has a well-proportioned and powerful body with a large, blunt triangle of a head with defined stop. Ears, small, erect; eyes, dark brown; tail, curls over.

Height: 61-71cm (24-28in).
Weight: 35-40kg (77-88lb).
Coat: harsh, straight outer, and dense, soft under.
Colour: any colour and combination.
Characteristics Intelligent, adaptable, good with children and faithful, it makes a good family dog requiring early discipline, moderate exercise and regular grooming.

The JAPANESE SHIBA is smaller than the Akita, with the typical sturdy spitz appearance, and is a popular family dog in Japan.

118

Toy Dogs

AFFENPINSCHER

History One of the oldest of the European toy terriers, it is the likely ancestor of both the Griffon Bruxellois and the Miniature Schnauzer.

Appearance Sturdy in body, it has a round, domed head with short, pointed muzzle. Ears, pointed, erect; eyes, round, dark; tail, carried high.

Height: 26cm (10in).

Weight: 3kg (7lb).

Coat: hard, wiry, long and shaggy on head.

Colour: usually black, sometimes red, or gray or black and tan.

Characteristics Alert, intelligent and affectionate, it can be quite an aggressive guard and needs discipline. It requires moderate exercise, minimum grooming.

GRIFFON BRUXELLOIS/ BRUSSELS GRIFFON/ BRABANÇON/ BELGIAN GRIFFON

History Developed in Belgium during the 19th century, there are three variations determined by colour and coat, very occasionally appearing in a single litter. Its ancestry of small street and stable dogs, affenpinscher and Pug produced a fearless little guard.

Appearance Strong and stocky, its head is monkey-like and round with deep stop and short, turned up nose. Ears, semi-erect, cropped in some countries; eyes, large, round, dark; tail, commonly docked.

Height: 20cm (8in).

Weight: 1.8-4.5kg (4-10lb).

Coat: rough, harsh, wiry with soft under coat and profuse beard (Bruxellois and Belgian); (Brabançon) smooth, short and close.

Colour: clear red, black, grizzle, or black and tan, or rusty red and black mixed, depending on variety.

Characteristics Makes a faithful, playful companion, requiring moderate exercise, but needs careful grooming with attention to eyes and muzzle, and rough coats should be hand-stripped not trimmed. Can be difficult to breed.

119

PUG

History Originally called the
Dutch Pug when its popularity
spread into Europe from Holland
where it was developed, its
miniaturized Mastiff appearance
is likely to have originated from
Far Eastern ancestors.

Appearance Broad-chested,
compact and strong in body, it
has a large, round, wrinkled
head and short, blunt muzzle.
Ears, small, fold forward; eyes,

large, round, fairly prominent,
and dark; tail, twists round over
hip.

Height: 25.4-28cm (10-11in).
Weight: 6.3-8kg (14-18lb).
Coat: short, fine and soft.
Colour: silver, apricot, fawn or
black.

Characteristics Very
affectionate, obedient and gentle
it makes a good pet and
companion, requiring only
modest exercise and grooming.

LOWCHEN/LITTLE LION DOG

History This little dog has its
ancient origins in southern
Europe, but has only recently
achieved international popularity

Appearance It has a well-
proportioned body with a short
broad head. Ears, pendant; eyes
dark; tail, medium length, carried
high when alert.

Height: 20-35cm (8-14in).
Weight: 2-4kg (4-9lb).
Coat: long and wavy, often
clipped to give lion mane and
tail.
Colour: any solid or particolour
Characteristics Bright, lively
and affectionate, it makes a good
family pet requiring moderate
exercise, regular grooming and
specialist clipping if wanted.

BICHON FRISE/TENERIFE DOG

History Recorded over 300 years ago in France, and brought there from the Canary Islands possibly as early as the 14th century, it acquired high status as a pet in European courts, but then moved on to become a popular circus performer before returning to being a family pet in the 20th century.

Appearance Deep-chested and compact, its head is well-proportioned with a shortish muzzle. Ears, long, pendant; eyes, dark; tail, curled over.

Height: 30cm (11in).
Weight: 4kg (9lb).
Coat: medium, fine, silky and curly.
Colour: white.

Characteristics Intelligent, lively, affectionate and sociable, it makes a good pet requiring moderate exercise and very regular grooming with attention to the ears.

BOLOGNESE

History This Bichon-type dog was developed centuries ago in Bologna, and became popular in ruling Italian households in the Renaissance.

Appearance It has a square, compact body, medium length head and neat, straight muzzle. Ears, long, pendant; eyes, brown; tail, curls over.

Height: 25-30cm (10-12in).
Weight: 2.5-4kg (5½-9lb).
Coat: long, shaggy and curly.
Colour: white.
Characteristics Rather quiet-natured, independent, intelligent and affectionate, it is a delightful pet requiring moderate exercise and regular grooming with attention to ears.

121

CAVALIER KING CHARLES SPANIEL

History Developed in the 20th century in England, this breed quickly established itself internationally. It is a larger, straighter-muzzled close cousin of the King Charles.

Appearance Has a well-proportioned, moderately deep-chested body, and a flat head with nicely tapered jaws. Ears, long, pendant; eyes, round, dark; tail, gently curves, or sometimes docked.

Height: 28cm (11in).

Weight: 5.4-8kg (12-18lb).

Coat: flat, silky, quite long, with feathering.

Colour: black and tan, ruby, Blenheim (white and chestnut), or tricolour.

Characterisics Calm, friendly and quite sporty, it makes a good family pet requiring plenty of exercise and regular grooming with attention to ears.

KING CHARLES SPANIEL/ENGLISH TOY SPANIEL (TOP)

History Descended and named from the breed that was a favourite of Charles II, though toy spaniels were recorded centuries before then and probably originated in China, it is sometimes identified by colour.

Appearance Compact and deep-chested, its head is domed with a short, slightly upturned nose. Ears, long, pendant; eyes, large, round, dark; tail, curves.

Height: 25cm (10in).

Weight: 3.5-6.3kg (8-14lb).

Coat: quite long, silky, slightly wavy, and feathering.

Colour: black and tan; tricolour (Prince Charles); chestnut-red (Ruby); red and white (Blenheim)

Characterisics Appealing and affectionate, it makes a good family pet requiring moderate exercise to avoid overweight, and regular grooming with attention to the ears.

PAPILLON AND PHALENE/CONTINENTAL TOY SPANIEL

History The small spaniels of Europe go back several centuries, and were popular pets in court circles in the 17th century.

Appearance Rather long-bodied, but well-balanced, they have a slightly domed head, distinct stop and finely pointed muzzle. Ears, large, erect (Papillon) or drop-eared (Phalene); eyes, round, dark; tail, plumed and arched over back.

Height: 20-28cm (8-11in).
Weight: 4-4.5kg (9-10lb).
Coat: long, flat, and silky, with distinct feathering.
Colour: white with patches of any colour except liver, or tricolour; the white, central blaze is distinctive.
Characteristics Easy to train, adaptable, they make active, loyal companions, benefitting from plenty of exercise and regular grooming.

MALTESE

History This type of dog was recorded in Phoenician times in 1000BC, and then as now they were kept as pets and companions. It only acquired its name and formal recognition in the 19th century.

Appearance It has a short, well-balanced, muscular body and a well-proportioned head with distinct stop. Ears, long, pendant; eyes, dark; tail, arches over back.

Height: 21-25cm (8-10in).
Weight: 1.8-2.7kg (4-6lb).
Coat: long, silky, straight, and well-feathered.
Colour: white.
Characteristics Loyal, lively and affectionate, it makes a good pet requiring only moderate exercise, but considerable grooming – its coat should not be allowed to get wet. Prefers a warm environment.

123

PEKINGESE

History This dog of the Chinese Imperial Palace was recorded in the Tang Dynasty. They were not seen outside the Palace until some were plundered by servicemen during the 1860 rebellion and brought to England.

Appearance Deep-chested and substantially built, it has a large, broad head and flat, wide, wrinkled muzzle. Ears, pendant; eyes, large, fairly prominent, dark; tail, curves over back.

Height: 15-23cm (6-9in).
Weight: 3.6-5kg (8-11lb).

Coat: long, profuse outer coat, soft under, and abundant feathering.

Colour: all colours and particolours.

Characteristics Affectionate, loyal and rather assertive, these surprisingly sporty little dogs make good pets when well-trained. They require only moderate exercise, but careful grooming with particular attention to eyes and face. The squashed nose can cause breathing difficulties and puppies should be bought with care.

POMERANIAN

History Bred down from the large Spitz dogs of the Arctic regions including the Samoyed, it was developed in the Pomeranian region of Germany and then further refined to its present size and colour range.
Appearance Compact and sturdy, it has a flat, wedge-shaped head and fine muzzle. Ears, small, erect; eyes, dark brown; tail, lies straight over back.
Height: 30cm (12in).
Weight: 1.8-2.5kg (4-5½lb).
Coat: profuse, straight, harsh outer coat, and soft, dense under.
Colour: all solid colours.
Characteristics Adaptable to almost any environment, it makes a quiet, well-behaved, loyal companion requiring modest exercise, but regular grooming.

JAPANESE CHIN/JAPANESE SPANIEL/TCHIN

History Whether the Chin or Pekingese came first is lost in Chinese history, but the Chin was introduced to Japan well over 1,000 years ago and has remained largely unaltered.
Appearance Compact and dainty, it has a round head, and short wide muzzle. Ears, medium length, fall forward; eyes, large, round, dark; tail, curls over.
Height: up to 22cm (9in).
Weight: 1.8-3.1kg (4-7lb).
Coat: long, dense, soft and silky with profuse feathering.
Colour: white with black markings, or with red, sable, brindle or lemon markings.
Characteristics Intelligent and docile, it is an affectionate family pet, requiring modest exercise, but regular and careful grooming.

YORKSHIRE TERRIER

History Bred for ratting in northern England in the mid 19th century, it is likely that it includes the old Black and Tan and Maltese Terriers in its ancestry.
Appearance Compact and muscular, it has a small, flatish head and firm straight muzzle. Ears, v-shaped, erect (occasionally semi-erect); eyes, dark; tail, commonly docked.
Height: 23cm (9in).
Weight: up to 3.2kg (7lb).
Coat: long, straight, fine and silky, non-shedding.
Colour: dark steel blue on body and tail, the rest bright tan.
Characteristics This is a hardy, bright and intelligent little dog with a playful and determined nature. It makes a popular and adaptable pet and a sometimes over-vociferous watch dog. It enjoys regular exercise, and coat demands considerable care to keep it tangle- and mat-free; non-show dogs are often trimmed.

MINIATURE PINSCHER

History Pinschers or terriers
have a long history in Germany.
The Miniature was standardized
in the late 19th century.
Appearance An elegant, sturdy
and well-balanced little dog with
a flat rather elongated head and
strong muzzle. Ears, smallish
either erect or dropped, cropped
in some countries; eyes, dark;
tail, commonly docked.
Height: 25.4-30cm (10-12in).
Weight: 4.5kg (10lb).
Coat: hard, short and glossy.
Colour: black, blue, or
chocolate, with defined tan
markings, or solid red.
Characteristics Easily trained,
active, and intelligent, it makes a
faithful companion and pet. It
enjoys plenty of exercise, but
requires only light grooming.

AUSTRALIAN SILKY TERRIER

History Bred from the
Australian and Yorkshire Terrier
in the mid 19th century, it was
first known as the Sydney Silky.
Appearance Deep-chested with
a long, sturdy body, it has quite
a long head and sturdy jaws.
Ears, small, v-shaped, erect; eyes
dark; tail, commonly docked.
Height: 23cm (9in).
Weight: 4.5-5kg (10-11lb).
Coat: long, fine and silky.
Colour: blue, or gray-blue with
tan markings.
Characteristics A very active,
intelligent and sociable dog, it
makes a lively companion,
though it can be pugnacious if
not firmly trained when young.
requires regular exercise and
very regular, gentle grooming to
prevent coat from matting. Some
owners will trim.

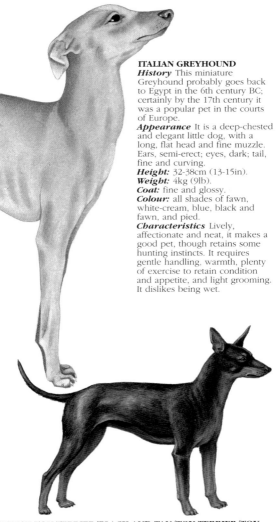

ITALIAN GREYHOUND

History This miniature Greyhound probably goes back to Egypt in the 6th century BC; certainly by the 17th century it was a popular pet in the courts of Europe.

Appearance It is a deep-chested and elegant little dog, with a long, flat head and fine muzzle. Ears, semi-erect; eyes, dark; tail, fine and curving.

Height: 32-38cm (13-15in).

Weight: 4kg (9lb).

Coat: fine and glossy.

Colour: all shades of fawn, white-cream, blue, black and fawn, and pied.

Characteristics Lively, affectionate and neat, it makes a good pet, though retains some hunting instincts. It requires gentle handling, warmth, plenty of exercise to retain condition and appetite, and light grooming. It dislikes being wet.

NGLISH TOY TERRIER/BLACK AND TAN/TOY TERRIER/TOY ANCHESTER TERRIER

istory Bred in England in the th century from the original anchester or Black and Tan rrier probably with Italian eyhound.

pearance A compact, deep-ested dog, it has a flat, wedge-aped head. Ears, flame-shaped, ct; eyes, dark; tail, tapering.

eight: 25-30cm (10-12in).

eight: 2.7-3.6kg (6-8lb).

Coat: dense, fine, close and glossy.

Colour: ebony black with very specific rich tan markings.

Characteristics Retaining its terrier character, this robust little dog makes an intelligent companion, requiring reasonable exercise, light grooming, and warmth and protection from wet or windy conditions.

CHINESE CRESTED DOGS

History Known in Central and South America in the 16th century, it is uncertain whether these unusual dogs – there are two varieties – are native or came from China, Africa or central Asia.

Appearance Small and sturdy, they have a broad head with distinct stop and long muzzle. Ears, pointed, erect; eyes, dark; tail, long, tapering.

Height: 30cm (12in).

Weight: 4.5kg (10lb).

Coat: skin is fine and silky with flowing tufts of hair only on head, tail and feet (Hairless); or covered with long soft hair (Powder Puff).

Colour: any colour, plain, spotted, or combinations.

Characteristics Affectionate, active, quiet and clean, these curious dogs make good companions requiring minimum exercise, but to be kept warm.

CHIHUAHUA: LONG AND SMOOTH COAT

History Believed to have been a sacred animal in Aztec times in Mexico and South America, it arrived in the USA in the late 19th century. The two varieties are alike except for their coats.

Appearance They are deep-chested, tiny dogs with a domed head, distinct stop and short pointed muzzle. Ears, large, wide, erect; eyes, round, dark or ruby; tail, tapers and curls up and over.

Height: 16-22cm (6-9in).

Weight: up to 2kg (6lb).

Coat: long coat is soft and slightly wavy with feathering; smooth coat is close and soft.

Colour: any colour or mixture.

Characteristics Quite fearless, they are not too good with dogs other than their own kind or with rowdy children. They are popular pets being bright, lively, affectionate little companions, though can be noisy and fussy feeders. They thrive on plenty of attention, limited exercise, and minimum grooming. (Molera, where the skull plates are not properly joined, is allowed in this breed.)

Dog First Aid

It is important to find a reliable and accessible veterinarian for your dog or puppy before and not after you acquire it. If you live in a town you may have several to choose from, and they are more likely to deal only with small animals, but if you live in a country area you may have little choice. Ask around for recommendations, go and meet the veterinarian and if you feel happy with the practice, discuss the dog you are getting, book in for a check-up within a 48-hour period of collecting your dog, ascertain the schedule for vaccinations, check up on the proposed diet for the dog, ask advice on insurance policies, and get a list of fees, charges for vaccinations, surgery times and emergency phone numbers.

Certain breeds of dog are either predisposed to a number of health problems, or through serious inbreeding, or through the on-breeding of congenital defects, will suffer minor or major problems some of which may not be diagnosable in young puppies. Only rigorous checks on the breeding lines of pedigree puppies can protect you against the sadness of having to put to sleep an otherwise fine young dog or having to maintain expensive treatment throughout its reduced life. Most well bred puppies will and should be vital, healthy and happy pets.

Throughout this section a * indicates a disorder that may either be congenital or to which certain breeds or types of dog are predisposed by breed formation.

Bright eyes, a damp, cold nose, good coat condition, healthy appetite and lithe movement are all indications of good health; symptoms of ill health are often equally obvious, but even slight problems can indicate the onset of something serious, so it is essential to consult your veterinarian immediately you perceive anything unusual. Reduced or no appetite, discharge from the eyes, bad breath, dribbling, dull coat condition, loss of hair, runny nose, shivering, coughing, sneezing, constant swallowing, frequent vomiting, diarrhea, excessive drinking, very dark urine, blood in the urine or faeces, lameness, head shaking, and ear scratching are all signs to watch for. Dogs can suffer from very serious, often fatal, contagious or infectious diseases, internal and external parasites, injury, inherited conditions, and indeed many of the conditions and diseases that humans are heir to. You, the owner can do a lot to prevent problems by maintaining vaccinations, by providing a properly balanced diet and adequate exercise, and as far as possible avoiding likely sources of infection.

The following entries cover most of the eventualities you may have to deal with, but the golden rule to follow is, if in any doubt, consult your veterinarian.

When your dog has been treated by the veterinarian, you may have to give it some form of medication yourself over a period of time. You may well have to provide additional warmth, and a hot waterbottle is useful if filled with hot, but not boiling, water and well wrapped in a blanket before being placed in the dog's bed. You should be given instructions about how to ensure that your dog drinks an adequate amount of water and eats a special diet, and when you are it is very important that you follow them exactly. When a dog is regularly handled and groomed, it is usually not difficult to give medication, whether it be eye or ear drops, pills or liquid medicine, and you should warmly praise it when it has kept still for you to do whatever is necessary. However, some dogs may wriggle and squirm and then it is useful to have someone else help you to hold the dog firmly but gently with the head still for eye or ear drops, or for liquid to be "injected" into the side of the mouth. (An unbreakable syringe – without a needle, of course – is invaluable for this as you can measure the exact dose; so ask your veterinarian for one.) Tablets rarely create

Areas around the eyes are cleaned gently with a soft, damp pad.

The visible areas only of the ear are cleaned monthly with lightly oiled cotton buds.

a problem if presented wrapped up in a tasty morsel of food, but if that does not work you will have to open the jaw and hold it open while you pop the pill into the back of the mouth, then hold it closed firmly while stroking down the throat to stimulate swallowing. You do need to make sure the pill has been swallowed as some dogs are very clever at holding them in their mouths and waiting until you are not watching to spit them out again.

First aid for dogs, whether for major or minor incidents, is largely a matter of commonsense. It is wise to keep a box

of basic dressings, blunt ended scissors, etc. ready to hand. And if you are in any doubt about what to do telephone a veterinarian and follow exactly the advice given.

Administering ear drops

Administering liquid medication using syringe without needle.

130

Administering eye drops

ACCIDENTS

Road accidents are all too common. If the animal is unconscious, it should be moved on a makeshift stretcher to a safe place or into a car with the minimum of disturbance and its airway cleared by pulling the tongue forward and removing any visible blockage, such as blood. Cover it with something warm to reduce the effects of shock, and call for, or preferably take it to a veterinarian. A wounded animal may need to be restrained as it is very likely to bite in self-defence anyone who approaches it. Make a noose with a leash, belt or piece of rope, approach the animal very quietly, talking reassuringly and slip the noose over the head as a makeshift muzzle and keep the animal still and quiet until professional help is found. Severe bleeding should be staunched with makeshift pressure pads. You will not know whether the dog has suffered internal injury – ruptures or broken bones – so all you can do will be to try and prevent any unnecessary movement.

Grazes, bites or cuts if at all deep should be dressed and treated by a veterinarian, but superficial grazes can be cleaned and dressed by you with insecticidal, antiseptic powder until healed. But infection can be passed on through any wound that breaks the skin, and even small holes can hide large areas of damaged tissue beneath the skin, so it is wise to consult your veterinarian.

Insect bites and stings can set up an allergic response, and when affecting the tongue or throat may cause breathing difficulties, occasionally even suffocation, and veterinary advice should be sought immediately if any aggravated responses are perceived. Usually, however, the pain or irritation can be alleviated with a cold compress. If possible remove any stings left behind with tweezers.

A makeshift muzzle can be made from a coat belt or a leash. If the dog is very distressed one person will be needed to keep it still enough for the muzzle to be tied on by another. It is wise to wear gloves if any are to hand.

131

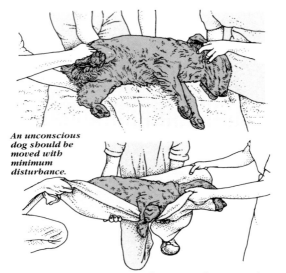

An unconscious dog should be moved with minimum disturbance.

Snakebites are not easy to diagnose unless you witnessed the event. If you suspect a poisonous bite, keep the dog as still as possible to reduce spread of poison and phone your veterinarian with description of snake.

Burns should also be treated professionally, but you can ease the pain for the animal by gently dousing the area with water and then a cold, wet cloth. Burns heal slowly.

Splinters of bone, glass, wood, or even sharp little seeds quite commonly get into or between the pads of the feet. If you can see them, use tweezers to remove them and apply antiseptic powder, but if the dog continues to limp and lick its foot then you will need professional help. Any foreign body that gets stuck in the throat or air passage will cause the dog to choke and gag, and will need to be dealt with immediately by the veterinarian. Some items may pass harmlessly through the digestive system. Puppies particularly, will try to eat almost anything. If something gets stuck in the mouth, you may be able to tweak it out but if it gets stuck further down and causes gagging and choking, you must take the dog for treatment.

Heatstroke is usually the result of a dog being left in an unventilated car in hot weather and causes a dog to collapse, pant excessively and froth at the mouth. Even if is unconscious, it should be doused with cold water immediately and then rushed to the nearest veterinarian.

Convulsions or fits may be caused by epilepsy or trauma. And unless the dog is known to be epileptic, seek professional advice immediately. During the fit, the dog should be prevented from injuring itself, cleaned up afterwards and given access to water but not food.

Drowning if treated promptly can result in complete recovery, so it is worth while knowing what you can do if faced with this emergency. Small dogs can be held upside down by the back legs and swung gently round to empty the lungs of water, and then, while still upside-down, have their chests pumped evenly to get air moving in and out. Once breathing starts, lay the dog down flat, keep it warm and take it to the veterinarian. Large dogs cannot be picked up like this without damage, so lift the hindquarters and support them on your shoulder or a ledge to get the head well below the chest, then pump the chest cavity to expel the water and encourage breathing to restart.

Poisoning may result in severe vomiting, sometimes with blood, general collapse, or fits. If you suspect what your dog has eaten take a sample with you and get the dog to a veterinarian with all speed.

Trapped underground is a situation most commonly experienced by small hunting dogs chasing prey down holes and then being unable to retreat. If you have suitable implements (spade), the terrain is penetrable and you can hear where the dog is, you can carefully dig it out. Otherwise, mark the ground surface both where you can hear the dog and the entry hole, and seek assistance from the local police. Army units, fire brigades and other human rescue services have all been known to help recover dogs in this situation.

PARASITES

External parasites that cause problems for dogs are fleas, ticks, mites and lice.

Fleas are very common and unless you have keen eyesight are not easily seen, but if you part the coat and examine the skin you may see flea droppings in the form of tiny black pinheads, and their presence will be obvious when your dog starts scratching. They should be dealt with immediately and you can do this yourself using one of the effective proprietary brands of spray or powder and following the instructions carefully – some are not suitable for puppies or bitches with puppies. Flea collars and insecticidal shampoos are also effective, but these are not always suitable. Some dogs develop allergies to flea bites, and this can be a problem if fleas are endemic in your garden for instance. Then, your only course of action is to maintain a regular course of deinfestation under the direction of your veterinarian.

Ticks are usually discovered as little lumps on the dog's skin when you are grooming, and are much more easy to see on smooth-coated dogs. They rarely cause much irritation to the dog, but they must be removed with a specific spray to ensure that the blood-sucking head buried in the skin comes away too or the site may go septic. Ticks can transmit serious diseases and must be dealt with as soon as they are discovered.

Dog First Aid

Mites come in many varieties. They attack the skin and ears. Most cause considerable irritation to the dog and if left untreated some will generate serious skin disorders that can be transmitted to humans. Immediately you suspect mites take your dog to the veterinarian who will take skin samples to establish which variety of mite it is before prescribing treatment.

Lice are very specific to their hosts and are rarely found on adult dogs, more often on puppies. You can usually detect them by the little white eggs (nits) visible on the hair. They are not dangerous and regular treatment with prescribed medication will soon despatch them.

Internal parasites that affect dogs are worms and protozoa. You need to ensure your dog remains free of them, and for some forms specific preparations are easily available with frequency and level of dosages clearly stated. However, the environment in which you live will dictate the level of reinfection, so it is worth asking your veterinarian for control dosages that are specifically relevant to your situation.

Roundworms are very common and can be seen in vomit or faeces. They can cause damage particularly to puppies and affect the intestinal tract and the lungs. Regular dosing is essential.

Tapeworms are transmitted through eating infected offal, prey or fleas, and can be detected by the rice-like segments that are visible in the faeces or around the anus. The dog will often show increased appetite, but a decrease in weight and general health. Again regular dosing is essential.

Lungworms, as their name implies, infect the lungs and cause a dry cough in the dog. Professional identification and treatment is essential.

Tracheal worms give rise to a similar cough as lungworms and again professional advice must be sought.

Hookworms, and there are two varieties, are associated with crowded, insanitary conditions. The larvae enter the body via the feet and through the mouth and can set up severe irritation. One usually stays in the feet, but the other lives in the intestine and can cause anaemia and general debility, even death. Veterinary treatment at the earliest sign is essential.

Heartworms are transmitted by mosquitos and are not found in Britain, and, as the name suggests, infect the vessels around the heart or the heart itself. If left untreated they will prove deadly. They are found only in hotter climates, but where they are known to exist preventative dosing regularly throughout the dog's life is essential. When taking a dog overseas, it is important to contact a veterinarian immediately on arrival.

Whipworms are not found in Britain but are common in some countries, and can be difficult to diagnose. They cause debilitating enteritis, and often fatal haemhorraging. Preventative dosing is essential.

134

Parasitic protozoa – and there are many varieties – are more common in hot countries. Symptoms can vary from diarrhea to other forms of debility, and infection via bitches to foetal puppies can cause serious defects. Clinical tests only will establish protozoan infestation followed by specifically prescribed treatments.

SKIN DISEASES

Accurate diagnosis of a particular skin disorder can only be made by a veterinarian. Early symptoms are often confusingly similar to parasitic infestation or hormonal problems: scurfy patches, hair loss, irritation, and so on. Each disease will respond to specific treatment, though some, such as allergies, are often difficult to diagnose and treat. The main skin diseases are mange, excema, allergies, and ringworm. *Ringworm* is highly infectious to humans and other animals. A fungal disease (not a worm) it can be recognized because of the circular patches it sets up on the skin and coat. Dogs with loose, deeply folded skin are susceptible to fungal and other skin problems and require very careful grooming.

EYE DISEASES

Dogs suffer from many of the eye diseases that afflict humans – conjunctivitis, glaucoma, cataracts, etc. – and the symptoms are similar: runny eyes, pale mucous membranes, unnatural discharge, milky corneas, swollen eyes and so on. Professional diagnosis is essential because, just as with humans, these symptoms can relate to other diseases such as diabetes. Any eye injury must be dealt with by a veterinarian, though you may find you can wash out a foreign body with a mild saline solution. However, some of the most serious eye problems that affect dogs are congenital defects which will not necessarily manifest themselves until the dogs have reached adulthood. Blindness may result from old age, previous eye disorders, cataracts or *Progressive Retinal Atrophy* (PRA) where inherited abnormalities in the retinal structure cause severely restricted or total loss of vision. PRA is presented in two forms – central or generalized – and is known to affect certain purebreeds. Good breeders will supply copies of PRA certificates for both parents of puppies from susceptible breeds. *Collie Eye Anomoly* (CEA), which affects predominantly Collies and Shetland Sheepdogs, can lead to detached retina or retinal haemorrhage and often blindness.

Congenital eye problems that cause severe irritation and often permanent damage are: *entropion* where the eyelid turns in; *ectropion* where the eyelid turns out; *trichiasis* where the eyelashes grow in the wrong direction; *distichiasis* where there are two rows of eyelashes; *narrow tear ducts* causing weeping; *luxation or dislocation of the eye lens*; *luxation of the eyeball*; *third eyelid deformities* such as *scrolled cartilage* and *prolapsed nictitans gland.* Some of these problems can be successfully treated if dealt with before the eye is permanently damaged. Another genetic problem affecting eyesight concerns *merle* dogs – those with a blue or pale eye and merles with two "normal" dark eyes. A cross of two dogs carrying the dominant merle gene will generate puppies that have to be destroyed at birth. (Merle dogs have a blue-gray coat normally streaked or ticked and this is commonly seen in Collies and Sheepdogs.)

EAR PROBLEMS
Deafness, as with humans, occurs quite commonly in older dogs, or it can be caused by an untreated infection or infestation. The signs will be a seeming disobedience to spoken commands and a general lack of responsiveness. You should have the dog checked by a veterinarian, and if the condition is untreatable you will need to provide your dog with more overt physical and visual attention and love. *Hereditary deafness* will also be irreversible and tends to affect white animals, and these dogs too will need special care and training.

Ear infections are more common in dogs with long floppy ears like the Spaniels and Poodles and in dogs that have skin problems, but can and do occur in all dogs. The symptoms will be ear-scratching, head shaking, rubbing the ears on the ground or against hard objects, and sometimes a nasty smell. The inflammation can be caused by parasites, bacteria, and micro-organisms such as fungi, a build up of wax or, particularly in summer months, little seeds from grasses or other plants down inside the canal. Only close examination by a veterinarian will determine the cause or combination of causes, and treatment – usually drops – may take quite a long time. But, as soon as you observe any symptoms you must take action quickly to avoid permanent damage.

Regular checking of your dog's ears helps to prevent or reduce the effects of infection. You can remove wax build up and knotted hair with gentle cleaning with a cotton bud dipped in luke-warm cod liver oil and pinching out the dead hair with your fingers. But never probe into any part of the ear you cannot see – that is for the professionals.

MOUTH PROBLEMS
Bad breath, gum problems, and loose teeth are the main problems associated with the mouth, though insect bites quite commonly affect the lips, mouth and tongue. Bad breath can be caused by digestive disorders, kidney problems, infected gums, or simply the consumption of rotten garbage. Some breeds seem to be more prone to than others, and your veterinarian will advise you if there anything you can do to improve the situation.

Gum problems are usually caused by a build up of tartar on the teeth and the setting up of *gingivitis* followed b loose teeth and gum abscesses. Puppy teeth not falling out naturally, or adult teeth not growing through properly will also cause gum inflammation and veterinary attention should be sought.

Tartar build up, when it occurs, taints the teeth brown and may be dealt with by including hard biscuits in the diet, by regular brushing using a canine toothpaste, or the teeth may need to be regularly scaled under anaesthetic by a veterinarian. If an *abscess* developes – a hard painful swelling – seek immediate professional attention as it will have to be drained and sometimes a tooth extracted.

It is possible to clean dogs' teeth with specially prepared canine toothpaste and a firm, soft toothbrush. The toothpaste is not always easily available, but if the practice is started young enough, the dog quite enjoys the procedure.

*Cleft and soft palates are inherited malformations. Puppies may well not survive, and dogs with either condition should not be used for breeding.

VOMITING

A dog will vomit quite naturally, sometimes a whole meal, and sometimes just froth, from eating a meal too quickly, from eating grass, or from eating something rotten. Persistent vomiting – more than five times in a few hours – or blood in the vomit, however, are symptoms of a variety of more serious problems including poisoning when veterinary advice should be sought immediately. If you suspect poison, take a sample of what the dog has recently eaten with you.

Gastritis and ***gastric torsion*** may also be indicated by persistent vomiting. Gastric torsion or gastric dilation, where the stomach becomes taught, distended and obviously painful, can occur in larger, deep-chested dogs that bolt down a big meal after energetic exercise and it will be fatal if not treated immediately by a veterinarian. Even then, the cure rate is low. Any dog with a suddenly swollen stomach must be taken to a veterinarian.

DIARRHEA

Persistent diarrhea may be a symptom of several problems, and any sign of blood in the faeces is likely to be serious. In both cases, seek veterinary advice.

A swelling in the anal region and the dog rubbing its bottom along the ground is a sign of blockage of the anal glands. Your veterinarian will need to deal with this problem, though if it occurs frequently you can learn how to deal with it yourself.

URINARY PROBLEMS

Very dark urine, blood in the urine, any evidence of discomfort when urinating, over-frequent urinating are all symptoms that require veterinary attention. Kidney infection or failure, diabetes, cystitis, stones in the bladder, hepatitis and incontinence could be causes and laboratory tests are called for.

Incontinence may signal a malfunction requiring professional attention, or may be the result of poor housetraining, or simply nervous excitement after periods of being left alone. In these last two instances the remedy is with you. (See page 41).

BREATHING DIFFICULTIES

Shortness of breath, excessive panting without obvious cause, lassitude, and dry coughing are indicators of heart and lung problems. You will not be able to tell which, but your veterinarian will. Coughing is also a symptom of some highly contagious diseases, so you should isolate your dog from other animals, and advise your veterinarian of the condition before you visit him or her so that they can make arrangements for your dog to be seen away from other animals in the surgery.

MUSCLE AND BONE PROBLEMS

Damage through injury can cause sprains, dislocation and breakages. Any loss of normal movement or limping should be reported to your veterinarian whether your dog is in obvious pain or not, and most of the problems are treatable. However there are problems affecting bones and muscles that are inherited and affect particular breeds of dogs, and some that are directly caused by bad nutrition in puppyhood.

Hip dysplasia is a seriously debilitating orthopedic problem, where the dog's hip joints fail because they do not fit properly. In some breeds the condition is quite common but is rarely evident in young puppies and in adult dogs (over 12 months) is confirmed by X-rays. Surgical treatment can improve the situation for some dogs. Good breeders should not supply puppies of affected breeds, and should supply screening certificates for both parent dogs.

Osteochondritis dissecans is more common in large breeds and is caused by cartilage failure in the shoulder and leg joints and the development of arthritis. Surgery can often improve the situation. Bad nutrition combined with fast growth in puppyhood is the common cause.

Arthritis is more commonly associated with old age in dogs and is treatable only with anti-inflammatory drugs. However, it can be caused by inherited anatomical faults and the damage is likely to be permanent.

Slipped discs or disc protrusion is not uncommon in dwarfed breeds with long backs and short legs where the spinal discs prematurely disintegrate and the spine is under more pressure. If your dog has an awkward posture or difficulty in movement then consult your veterinarian immediately – drugs or surgery may be indicated.

Cervical spondylopathy, where the spinal discs are malformed, is shown most commonly by a wobbl uncertain gait. X-rays will confirm the condition and early diagnosis may help with treatment, but often the condition is terminal.

Knee (stifle) and elbow problems that are caused by inherited weakness, over or undernutrition, or overstress in puppyhood include easily dislocated patellae and ruptured ligaments. These can be alleviated with surgical treatment and rest.

REPRODUCTIVE PROBLEMS

Many internal problems associated with the reproductive organs can only be diagnosed by your veterinarian. The symptoms to watch for are unusual discharge, difficulty in urinating, lumps or swellings on the testicles, sheath, or breasts, unusual thirst, lack of appetite, problems with defaecating and vomiting. Certain breeds, however, are more prone to problems.

Unilateral or bilateral cryptorchidism or partially or wholly undescended testicles is identifiable at about ten months and if not surgically attended to can lead to malignant growths. Dogs should not be bred from with this condition and cannot be shown.

Whelping difficulties are often associated with some of the toy breeds and breeds with flat noses.

False pregnancy is not uncommon and usually occurs about two months after heat. Bitches behave as if they are expecting puppies and physically their stomachs can swell and they can start producing milk. Consult your veterinarian on treatment to be applied.

OTHER INTERNAL DISORDERS

Digestive, respiratory, circulatory, neurological, urinary, and hormonal problems can all occur in dogs as they do in humans. And certain problems are linked to breed weaknesses or inherited malformations.

Incomplete tracheal cartilage rings can cause blockages in the airway.

Soft palate where an overlong palate can block the airway and cause difficult and noisy breathing. Surgery can sometimes alleviate the problem.

Exocrine pancreatic insufficiency (EPI) occurs where a malformed pancreas does not produce sufficient digestive juices for the dog to be nourished properly. Enzyme treatment is prescribed for the rest of the dog's life.

Diabetes is usually indicated by constant thirst and lethargy. Insulin treatment is normally given for the rest of the dog's life.

Epilepsy can be inherited, or be the result of trauma or other disease. Treatment is with drugs but the prognosis is usually poor.

Heart murmur in young dogs is caused by congenital weakness or malformation of the heart valves and is often indicated by a dry cough and general lethargy. In older dogs it can be caused by wear and tear or by infections that have damaged the valves, (e.g. from infected gums and teeth). *Vascular ring anomaly* is another condition caused by congenital heart malformation, and this affects swallowing. Drugs and surgery are the treatments available.

UNNATURAL WEIGHT GAIN/WEIGHT LOSS

While excessive weight, or underweight could be the result of too much or too little food, it can also be a sign of thyroid deficiency or some collapse in the digestive system. It is important therefore to seek professional advice.

CONTAGIOUS AND INFECTIOUS DISEASES

Rabies is transmitted to humans as well as dogs via saliva into the blood stream – most commonly through a cut or a bite. The rabies virus attacks the brain and the nervous system and is usually fatal. Carriers in the wild are foxes, wolves, racoons, skunks and others, and where the disease is endemic all domestic dogs must be inoculated. Once infected the dog will progress rapidly from minor behaviour alteration, to unprovoked aggression and drooling, to convulsions, to a coma, and then death. In humans the progression is similar. Any dog exhibiting symptoms must be reported to the police and local health departments.

In Britain rabies is eradicated and inoculations are not compulsory. Dogs brought in to those countries free of the virus have to go through stringent quarantine procedures.

Distemper also known as hardpad, is endemic in most countries. It is highly infectious, and symptoms can be that of a mild cold, which can develop later – two or three weeks – into serious illness with high temperature, sickness and diarrhea. While the dog may appear to recover, the virus remains in the system and can cause fits and paralysis. Puppies must have a course of vaccinations, but this can only start at eight to ten weeks, and until complete the puppy should be kept away from other dogs and public areas. Booster vaccinations should be maintained throughout the dog's life.

Infectious canine hepatitis is also very contagious, and can prove fatal within 24 hours of symptoms being obvious, although in less acute forms it will affect eyes, liver, kidneys and lungs. If a dog does recover it will remain a carrier and a threat to all other dogs. Early vaccination and maintenance boosters are essential for the control of this disease.

Canine parvovirus infection can cause heart damage in puppies, and persistent vomiting and severe diarrhea with bleeding in older dogs, and is usually fatal. It can be spread through indirect contact, on shoes and on clothes, is very contagious, and is resistant to most disinfectants (though strong solutions of bleach can be effective). The virus is now endemic practically worldwide and vaccination for puppies followed by boosters is essential.

140

eptospirosis There are two *leptospires* bacteria that infect dogs. *L.canicula* can cause death very quickly, or cause such serious kidney damage that death will occur a few years later. The bacterium is carried in the urine and can also infect humans. *L. icterohaemorrhagiae* is carried by rats and can be caught by swimming in water contaminated by rats' urine and is passed on to humans as well as dogs. It infects the liver causing jaundice, and in dogs, usually death. Prevention by vaccination starting in puppyhood is the only effective control.

OLD AGE

Do not expect your dog to retain the same level of vigour and energy as it reaches the end of its lifespan. Not only will appetite diminish, so that you will need to adjust to higher essential nutrient levels, but the problems of age will impinge to a greater or lesser degree – deafness, blindness, stiffening of the joints, less resistance to diseases affecting kidneys, digestion, heart, etc. Tumours that may or may not be operable can also occur. Of course, many dogs remain fit and active for the whole of their lives, but others will need more patience, love and care. Your dog may die suddenly and quite naturally, or you may have to have him euthanased. The decision to have your dog put to sleep is never easy, but your guiding rule must always be that if your pet is distressed and in pain and there is no more you or your veterinarian can do to make its life happy, then a painless injection to end its life is your only choice. The operation takes only a few seconds.

BREEDING

There is no room in a book of this size to examine the procedures involved in mating, pregnancy, and bitch and litter care. Individual breeds of dogs require different levels of care, and specialist books are available to all. Anyone planning to set up as a breeder, whether professionally or just for a single litter should study the subject in detail relating to their breed of dog.

There are, however, a few basic things that are useful to know right from the start. Most important of all, do not even consider breeding from your dog without first having screened to ensure that it is not going to pass on any genetic weakness or malformations to the puppies.

From successful mating, gestation averages about 63 days. Bitches require a special diet both during pregnancy, while they are suckling their puppies, and after the puppies are weaned. A bitch should have a specially constructed bed in which to have her puppies that allows her to get in easily and restrains the puppies from getting out. It should be set up in a warm, quiet, light place, with access to easily washable, but restrictable floor space where the puppies can play safely. Most bitches give birth naturally and manage well by themselves. However, all litters must be

supervised as they arrive and your veterinarian should b
on 24-hour call out should any emergency occur. You
veterinarian should inspect the litter within a few days
check their general health and, if necessary, to dock tai
and remove dew claws.

Weaning periods vary with the breed of dog, but th
must be done gradually allowing time for the bitch's mi
naturally to dry out, and for each of the puppies to learn
lap and eat their full dietary quota. Puppies' diets have to b
carefully worked out so that they receive an even
balanced diet given in several meals over a 24-hour perio
Looking after puppies is a fulltime job for both bitch ar
owner for about eight weeks.

INHERITED DEFECTS

Inherited characteristics of shape, colour, coat, etc. are wh
determine the accepted standards of individual breed
And, indeed, what may be considered a fault in one bree
may be a desirable feature in another. Certain pedigre
breeds, however, either because of their conformation
through poor breeding controls, can pass on to the
offspring certain weaknesses or defects that either in
minor or extremely serious manner can affect vitality ar
normal life expectation.

Different regulating bodies in different countries pursu
varying policies with regard to the control and eliminatio
of inherited defects in the pure breeds of dogs. Son
follow a national system binding upon all show ar
commercial dog breeders, others rely on individual bree
societies to maintain effective controls. Certainly form
schemes exist for screening some specific diseases. Th
problems have arisen over the years because sho
standards have sometimes encouraged exaggerated physic
characteristics detrimental to a particular breed's gene
viability, because swings in popularity have put pressur
on limited breed lines, and because unscrupulous breede
have bred from unsound stock. Regulating bodies, sho
judges, breeders and dog owning members of the pub
must all share the responsibility both for the situation as
is, and in rectifying it.

Individual dog owners can help by reporting cases
affected dogs to breed societies and regulating bodies,
ensuring they are provided with clean veterinary certifica
for the parent stock of a puppy, by reserving the right
reject a puppy that fails a full veterinary check within
hours of acquisition, and by not breeding from any dog
bitch that has a hereditary defect, however minor.

Index

Index